HEALTHMARK

Cooking
FOR A
Healthier
Ever After

SUSAN STEVENS, M.A., R.D.

HealthMark Centers, Inc.
Englewood, Colorado

Cooking for a Healthier Ever After

Acknowledgments

This book would not have been created without Dr. Rob Gleser's inspiration and his dedication to the HealthMark lifestyle.

My thanks to the many HealthMark alumni and to the HealthMark restaurants who so generously contributed favorite recipes.

And special thanks are due to the HealthMark staff and to my family, whose tastebuds helped ensure the success of each recipe.

Cover art by Gary Monaco; Cover design by Bill Coburn; Typesetting by A. Celeste Velasquez and John Cruise.

Additional copies of this book may be obtained by sending a check for $16.95* plus $2.50 shipping and handling to:

HealthMark Centers, Inc.
5801 South Quebec, Suite 100
Englewood, Colorado 80111
303/694-5060

*Colorado residents add $1.13 tax

Order blanks are included in the back of the book

Published by HealthMark Centers, Inc., Englewood, Colorado
Third Edition, November, 1990

ISBN # 0-9624784-1-5

Printed on recycled paper

Foreword

In 1985 the first HealthMark Center opened. Our corporate goal was to develop a successful preventive medicine program that, above all, had to be easy to live with. The success of over 10,000 graduates from our programs is testimony to the achievement of this goal.

From the nutrition aspect, the goal was to dispel the myth that health food had to look brown and taste bland. Enter Susan Stevens and "Voila" — it was done. Beyond any dispute we have achieved our goals.

Cooking for a Healthier Ever After is the basic introduction to the HealthMark style of cooking. This extremely successful cookbook was followed by the best seller, *Delitefully HealthMark,* both written by Ms. Stevens. In all, over 70,000 cookbooks have been sold making these books among the all time best sellers in the region — another testimony to the popularity of the HealthMark lifestyle.

Now this original introduction to HealthMark cooking has been redone with additional recipes, nutritional information for each recipe and an improved format for ease of use.

With both books in your recipe library you have a complete guide to healthy eating — deliciously!

Enjoy the best of health.

Rob Gleser, M.D.
Founder and Director
HealthMark Centers, Inc.

November, 1990

Table of Contents

Introduction

Welcome to cooking HealthMark style, the healthiest cooking around. The recipes in this book have all been selected and developed with your enjoyment as well as your health in mind. If the HealthMark style of cooking is new to you, then you are in for a treat as you will find the recipes convenient and easy to prepare as well as delicious.

Recipes in this book have been modified to be as low in fat (especially saturated fat), cholesterol, sodium and sugar as possible and still look and taste wonderful. This is gourmet food that enhances your health and well-being.

As you select ingredients, shop carefully to ensure that you are using the healthiest foods possible. Fresh, high-quality ingredients produce the best results.

When you are confident with these recipes and cooking techniques, modify your own favorite recipes. (The second HealthMark cookbook, *Delitefully HealthMark* tells you how.) You will soon find that you are creating new dishes as well!

— Bon Appetit
S.S.

HealthMark Dietary Goals

HealthMark is dedicated to helping people live a healthier, more active life and reduce — or eliminate — risk for various life-threatening diseases: heart disease, high blood pressure, stroke, adult onset diabetes and certain cancers. Good nutrition, regular exercise and stress management all play a role in improved health. The HealthMark Dietary Goals are designed to provide a framework for healthy eating habits:

1. Reduce fat consumption to 20% of total calories; limit fat intake to 45 grams per day.

The typical American diet contains 40% of calories from fat, an amount which is not compatible with good health. Trim your fat intake by eating leaner meats, cooking poultry without the skin, using non-fat dairy products and using less fat in cooking. Cutting down on snacks, frozen meals and processed foods as well as sweets and desserts will also help trim fat calories from your diet.

2. Reduce saturated fat consumption; replace saturated fats with monounsaturated and polyunsaturated fats (in small amounts).

Saturated fats are found in meat and dairy products as well as in certain vegetable oils. Coconut and palm oils are high in saturated fat and should be avoided. Liquid vegetable oils, such as soy, corn and cottonseed that have been hydrogenated have more saturated fat than in their natural form and should be avoided as much as possible.

Saturated fats, which usually are solid at room temperature (e.g. butter, meat fat), elevate blood cholesterol levels and increase risk for heart disease. Too much fat in the diet increases risk for certain cancers and provides excessive calories leading to overweight and obesity.

Some foods, such as meat and dairy products, contain both cholesterol and saturated fat, both of which elevate blood cholesterol. Other fats, such as coconut oil, palm oil, margarine and shortening (hydrogenated vegetable oils) have no cholesterol, but are still capable of raising blood cholesterol because of their saturated fat content.

It is important to remember that a food does not have to contain cholesterol to raise your blood cholesterol!

Avoid saturated fats by eating leaner meats, using non-fat dairy products and reading labels to avoid products that use coconut oil, palm oil or hydrogenated vegetable oils.

3. Limit dietary cholesterol to 150 mg. (or less per day).

Cholesterol is found only in foods of animal origin — meats, poultry, fish and seafood, dairy products and egg yolks. The same recommendations (above) that reduce fat intake will also reduce cholesterol consumption. Also, limit use of egg yolks as a single yolk contains

215 milligrams of cholesterol. Organ meats, such as liver, are also extremely high in cholesterol.

4. Reduce sodium intake to 2300 milligrams per day.

Many people experience high blood pressure when their diet is high in sodium. Reducing dietary sodium often brings high blood pressure under control.

Use less salt in cooking and remove the salt shaker from the table. Avoid chips, crackers and other snack foods as well as frozen and canned foods high in sodium — read the label to find out how much sodium is in a serving.

The good news is that your tastebuds will easily adjust to less salt and in a few weeks you won't even miss it.

5. Limit sugar and alcohol.

Both are empty calories, contributing many calories and few nutrients. Replace the sugary snacks, desserts and beverages with fresh fruit and juice. Drink alcohol in moderation — no more than two drinks a day, preferably less.

6. Increase complex carbohydrates and fiber.

Make pasta, potatoes, dried beans and peas, rice, cereals, whole grains, fresh vegetables and fruit the main focus of your diet. At least 50% to 60% of your calories should come from these complex carbohydrates.

Complex carbohydrates are digested gradually (unlike sugar, which enters and leaves the bloodstream quickly), providing you with a steady flow of energy. They are bulky, dense and filling, leaving you satisfied longer on fewer calories. Additionally, complex carbohydrates supply generous amounts of fiber, which is needed for regularity and, perhaps, cancer prevention. Fiber is the "roto-rooter" of your digestive tract.

Following these dietary recommendations will not only help you reduce your risk for eight of the leading causes of death in this country, but they will also help you attain and maintain your ideal weight. Along with a regular exercise program, good eating habits will give you more pep and energy, reduce fatigue and stress, and help you feel

HEALTHIER EVER AFTER!

Cook's Notes

- Add flavor to baked goods, sauces and other dishes by adding **zest,** the thin outer layer of an orange, lemon or other citrus peel. Use a zester (a tool available in cookware stores) or a grater to remove the zest.

- Fresh herbs have the best flavor, but if not available, substitute 1/2 to 1 tsp. dried herb per tablespoon of fresh herb. Give dried herbs a fresh taste by mixing with an equal amount of chopped fresh parsley, then let stand 10 to 15 minutes before using.

- Olive, canola and safflower are best choices for cooking oils. Use olive oil for sauteeing and salad dressings; choose canola or safflower for baking.

- Bake in non-stick pans coated with cooking spray or brush pan lightly with oil.

- Line muffin pans with paper liners to minimize clean-up.

- A 1/4 cup measure is just the right size for scooping muffin batter into a muffin cup.

- Muffins and other baked goods can easily be prepared in the food processor: measure dry ingredients into work bowl first and pulse until just blended; add nuts and/or dried fruit and pulse until chopped. Add liquid ingredients and pulse until batter is just blended.

- Microwave lemons and limes for 30 to 60 seconds before juicing.

- Honey is easier to measure when warmed.

- To substitute honey for sugar, decrease liquid in the recipe by 1/4 cup. If recipe has no liquid added, add 4 tablespoons flour. Decrease baking temperature by 25° to prevent over-browning.

- Measure oil first, then honey will slide easily out of the cup.

- If unsalted nuts are not available, rinse salted nuts then toast briefly before using.

- Eggs are easiest to separate when cold; the whites beat up to greatest volume at room temperature.

- If fresh orange juice is not available, substituted frozen orange juice concentrate — one tablespoon equals about 1/4 cup fresh juice.

- For best results, preheat oven before baking.

- Prick meat all over with a fork to allow marinade to penetrate thoroughly.

- To prevent skinless chicken from drying out, reduce cooking time by a few minutes.

- Wash poultry with warm water before using to decrease bacteria and minimize chance of illness. Be sure to wash hands, utensils, cutting board, sink and anything else that comes in contact with raw poultry.

Nutrition Analysis Information

Recipes have been computer analyzed for calories, fat, cholesterol, dietary fiber and sodium. Nutrition information is given for a single serving, based on the largest number of servings given for the recipe. For some recipes, serving size is specified.

Use this nutrition information to help you select recipes to meet and fit within the HealthMark Dietary Goals:

- 150 milligrams of dietary cholesterol

- 20 to 25 percent of calories from fat; not more than 45 grams of fat per day

- 2300 milligrams of sodium

- 25 to 35 grams of dietary fiber

Cooking for a Healthier Ever After

Chips

Homemade ("Fat-Free") Tortilla Chips 4
Pita Chips 4

Dips

Black Bean Dip 5
Chili Bean Dip 6
Curried Shrimp Dip 8
HealthMark Sour Cream 3
Hummus 10
Mexican Salsa 5
Popeye's Spinach Dip 7
Red Onion Dip 7
Rob's Cream Cheese 3
Tex-Mex Dip 6
Zesty Clam Dip 8

Spreads

Fresh Salmon Tartare 9
Smoked Salmon Spread 9

Other

Caponata 10
Crab Stuffed Mushrooms 12
Eggplant Caviar 11
HealthMark "Gorp" 13
Marinated Mushrooms 12

Rob's Cream Cheese

1 cup 1% cottage cheese

Puree cottage cheese in blender or food processor until smooth. Spoon into coffee filter or cheesecloth. Place in a strainer, then suspend over a bowl. Cover and place in refrigerator for 24 to 48 hours.

Excess moisture will drain and a creamy spread will remain. Use on bagels, toast, quick breads or as a base for dips.

Yield: 1 cup; 1 serving = 2 Tbsp.

Per serving:	Calories	Fat (g)	Cholesterol (mg)	Fiber (g)	Sodium (mg)
	21	0	0	0	117

HealthMark Sour Cream

Use this as a low-cal replacement for sour cream in dips

1 cup 1% cottage cheese　　　　**¹/4 cup non-fat yogurt, low-fat buttermilk**
1 Tbsp. lemon juice　　　　　　**or non-fat milk**

Puree all ingredients in blender or food processor until *very* smooth.

Use as a topping for baked potatoes. May also be substituted for mayonnaise in tuna or chicken salad.

Yield: About 1¹/4 cups; 1 serving = 2 Tbsp.

Per serving:	Calories	Fat (g)	Cholesterol (mg)	Fiber (g)	Sodium (mg)
	20	0	1	0	96

Homemade ("Fat-Free") Tortilla Chips

12 corn tortillas *or*
12 whole wheat flour tortillas
Water
Garlic, onion or chili powder (optional)

Brush tortillas one at a time with water. If desired, sprinkle lightly with garlic, onion or chili powder. Cut into six to eight wedges.

Arrange tortilla wedges on baking sheet coated with cooking spray. Bake at 425° for 5 to 7 minutes, turn and bake another 5 to 7 minutes or until crisp. Repeat until all chips are baked.

Yield: 72 to 96 pieces; 1 serving = 1 tortilla (6 to 8 pieces)

Per serving:	Calories	Fat (g)	Cholesterol (mg)	Fiber (g)	Sodium (mg)
	63	1	0	0	74

Pita Chips

4 whole wheat pita breads, split in half   **4 tsp. Parmesan cheese**
2 tsp. olive *or* **safflower oil**   **2 tsp. poppy** *or* **sesame seeds**

Brush pita bread lightly with oil. Sprinkle lightly with Parmesan, then with poppy or sesame seeds. Cut each into eight wedges. Arrange on a baking sheet. Bake at 350° until crisp, about 5 to 10 minutes.

Pita chips may also be prepared without oil. Cut into wedges, then bake until crisp.

Yield: 32 pieces; 1 serving = 4 pieces.

Per serving:	Calories	Fat (g)	Cholesterol (mg)	Fiber (g)	Sodium (mg)
	65	2	1	2	9

Mexican Salsa

2 or 3 green onions
2 cloves garlic, minced
1 28-oz. can salt-free whole tomatoes or
 5 to 6 fresh tomatoes, cored and chopped

1/4 cup chopped green chiles (or jalapeños)
1/4 cup chopped fresh cilantro
1 tsp. oregano
1/4 tsp. cumin

In a blender or food processor chop onions and garlic. Add remaining ingredients and process until coarsely chopped.

Use as a topping for baked potatoes, a dip for fresh vegetables or as a topping for grilled chicken or fish. Also serve with freshly made Tortilla Chips (page 4) or spooned over an egg white omelette.

Yield: about 2 cups; 1 serving = 2 Tbsp.

Per serving:	Calories	Fat (g)	Cholesterol (mg)	Fiber (g)	Sodium (mg)
	11	0	0	0	9

Black Bean Dip

1 onion, chopped
1 Tbsp. olive oil
1 clove garlic, minced
1 15-oz. can black beans, drained

1 tsp. celery seed, crushed
1 to 2 Tbsp. Worcestershire sauce
1/4 tsp. hot pepper sauce (optional)
Chopped fresh cilantro

Saute onion and garlic in olive oil until softened, but not brown, about 5 minutes. Cool slightly. Combine with beans and remaining ingredients in a food processor or blender. Process until smooth.

Pour into a saucepan and simmer over low heat for 15 to 25 minutes or until of dipping consistency.

Serve hot or cold garnished with chopped cilantro. Serve with Tortilla Chips (page 4) or fresh vegetables.

Yield: 1 1/2 cups; 1 serving = 2 Tbsp.

Per serving:	Calories	Fat (g)	Cholesterol (mg)	Fiber (g)	Sodium (mg)
	53	1	0	1	190

Tex-Mex Dip

3 ripe avocados, peeled
2 Tbsp. lemon juice
1/4 tsp. pepper
1 cup plain non-fat yogurt
1/2 cup light, cholesterol free mayonnaise
1 11/8-oz. pkg. taco seasoning mix
2 101/2-oz. cans jalapeño-flavored
   bean dip (no lard)

1 bunch green onions with tops, sliced
2 31/2-oz. cans pitted ripe olives, rinsed,
   drained and coarsely chopped
4 oz. low-fat cheddar cheese, shredded
Tortilla Chips (page 4)

In a medium-size bowl mash avocados with lemon juice and pepper. Combine yogurt, mayonnaise and taco seasoning mix in a small bowl.

To assemble: spread bean dip on a large, shallow serving platter; top with avocado mixture, then spread with yogurt mixture. Sprinkle with chopped onions, tomatoes and olives; cover with shredded cheese.

Serve chilled or at room temperature with Tortilla Chips (page 4).

Serves 24

Per serving:	Calories	Fat (g)	Cholesterol (mg)	Fiber (g)	Sodium (mg)
	117	9	5	1	419

Chili Bean Dip

1 15-oz. can salt-free pinto, kidney
   or black beans, drained *or*
   2 cups cooked beans
1 to 2 Tbsp. bean liquid
1 Tbsp. vinegar
1 tsp. chili powder (or more to taste)

1/4 tsp. *each* cumin and salt
1 clove garlic, minced
1/4 cup chopped onion
1 to 2 Tbsp. chopped fresh cilantro
1/4 cup chopped green chiles

Combine all ingredients, except green chiles, in a blender or food processor. Blend until smooth. Mix in green chiles.

Serve with warm Tortilla Chips (page 4), wedges of whole wheat pita bread or fresh vegetables (jicama is especially good).

Yield: about 2 cups; 1 serving = 2 Tbsp.

Per serving:	Calories	Fat (g)	Cholesterol (mg)	Fiber (g)	Sodium (mg)
	52	0	0	3	36

Popeye's Spinach Dip

1 10-oz. package frozen chopped spinach
1/4 to 1/3 package dry vegetable soup mix
2 cups plain non-fat yogurt
1/4 cup light, cholesterol-free
  mayonnaise

1 8-oz. can water chestnuts,
  drained and chopped
2 green onions, thinly sliced
1 clove garlic, minced
1 4- to 6-oz. can shrimp, rinsed and drained

Thaw spinach; drain and squeeze dry. Blend with remaining ingredients. Chill before serving. Serve with raw vegetables, such as celery, carrots, red, green or yellow pepper strips, jicama, broccoli or cauliflower florets.

For an attractive presentation, serve dip in a round loaf of sheepherders or sourdough bread. Slice top off loaf and hollow out center. Fill with chilled dip. Serve with bread cubes, whole wheat crackers and raw vegetables.

Yield: 3 cups; 1 serving = 2 Tbsp.

Per serving:	Calories	Fat (g)	Cholesterol (mg)	Fiber (g)	Sodium (mg)
	38	1	8	0	93

Red Onion Dip

1 red onion, minced
2 Tbsp. sugar *or* honey
2 Tbsp. red wine vinegar

1 tsp. chopped fresh dill
1 cup plain non-fat yogurt

Mix onion, sugar and vinegar. Let stand until onion is limp, about 30 minutes. Drain, pressing out excess liquid. Stir in dill.

Serve with cucumber sticks for dipping.

Yield: about 1 1/2 cups; 1 serving = 2 Tbsp.

Per serving:	Calories	Fat (g)	Cholesterol (mg)	Fiber (g)	Sodium (mg)
	30	0	1	0	17

Curried Shrimp Dip

1 zucchini, shredded
$1/2$ tsp. Lite Salt™
1 cup plain non-fat yogurt
$1/4$ cup thinly sliced green onions

$1/4$ lb. cooked small shrimp
$1/4$ cup chopped fresh cilantro
Dash Tabasco sauce

In a small bowl, toss zucchini with salt. Let stand until wilted, 20 to 30 minutes. Rinse and drain well, squeezing out as much liquid as possible.

Combine with remaining ingredients. Serve immediately or chill one hour before serving. Serve with raw vegetables such as: celery, jicama, cucumber or zucchini sticks.

Yield: about $2^1/2$ cups; 1 serving = 2 Tbsp.

Per serving:	Calories	Fat (g)	Cholesterol (mg)	Fiber (g)	Sodium (mg)
	17	0	9	0	25

Zesty Clam Dip

1 $6^1/2$-oz. can minced clams,
  rinsed and drained
1 cup Rob's Cream Cheese (page 3)

2 Tbsp. chopped fresh parsley
1 Tbsp. chopped onion
2 tsp. *each* lemon juice and horseradish

Drain clams reserving liquid. Add 3 Tbsp. clam liquid to Cream Cheese, beating until smooth. Blend in remaining ingredients. Serve with crisp raw vegetables.

Yield: $1^1/4$ cups; 1 serving = 2 Tbsp.

Per serving:	Calories	Fat (g)	Cholesterol (mg)	Fiber (g)	Sodium (mg)
	45	0	11	0	103

Smoked Salmon Spread

1 cup Rob's Cream Cheese (page 3)
1/2 cup canned salmon, rinsed,
  drained and flaked

1/4 cup minced red or green onion
1/2 tsp. liquid smoke

Blend all ingredients and chill well before serving.

Yield: about 1 1/2 cups; 1 serving = 2 Tbsp.

Per serving:	Calories	Fat (g)	Cholesterol (mg)	Fiber (g)	Sodium (mg)
	27	1	7	0	112

Fresh Salmon Tartare

2 lb. fresh salmon fillets, cut into chunks
1/4 cup minced fresh parsley
2 Tbsp. capers, rinsed and drained
2 Tbsp. chopped fresh chives

2 Tbsp. olive oil
3 Tbsp. fresh lemon juice
2 tsp. Dijon mustard
Dash hot pepper sauce

Coarsely chop salmon in food processor or by hand; do not puree. Transfer to a medium bowl and blend in parsley, capers and chives. In a separate bowl, whisk together oil, lemon juice, mustard and hot pepper sauce. Add to salmon and toss lightly; do not mash. Chill for 2 hours.

Serve with pumpernickel, black rye bread, or Pita Chips (page 4).

Yield: 3 cups; 1 serving = 1/4 cup

Per serving:	Calories	Fat (g)	Cholesterol (mg)	Fiber (g)	Sodium (mg)
	163	8	45	0	79

Caponata

1 large eggplant, diced
1 onion, sliced
1/4 cup olive oil
6 tomatoes, cored and diced
2 stalks celery including tops, diced

1/2 cup sliced black olives, rinsed and drained
2 Tbsp. capers, rinsed and drained
2 Tbsp. *each* sugar and red wine vinegar
1/2 tsp. pepper

Saute eggplant and onion in olive oil until lightly browned. Add tomatoes and celery. Cover and cook over low heat for 15 minutes. Add olives, capers, sugar, vinegar and pepper. Cover and simmer an additional 15 minutes. Chill before serving.

Serves 4 to 6

Per serving:	Calories	Fat (g)	Cholesterol (mg)	Fiber (g)	Sodium (mg)
	169	12	0	4	162

Hummus

1/4 cup sesame seeds *or* 2 Tbsp. tahini
1 15-oz. can garbanzo beans,
  rinsed and drained
3 Tbsp. lemon juice

1 Tbsp. olive oil
1 to 2 cloves garlic, minced
1/4 to 1/2 tsp. cumin (optional)

In a dry skillet toast sesame seeds, stirring frequently, until golden. Combine all ingredients in a food processor or blender and pulse on and off until well chopped. Then process for 30 to 45 seconds until light and fluffy. If mixture is too thick add water, one tablespoon at a time, until desired consistency.

Serve with whole wheat pita bread wedges, low-fat crackers, breadsticks or raw vegetables.

Yield: 2 cups; 1 serving = 2 Tbsp.

Per serving:	Calories	Fat (g)	Cholesterol (mg)	Fiber (g)	Sodium (mg)
	66	3	0	1	84

Eggplant Caviar

1 eggplant, about 2 lbs.
1/4 cup tahini
1/4 cup lemon juice
1 clove garlic, minced
1/4 cup chopped onion

1/4 tsp. cumin
1/4 tsp. salt
1/8 tsp. cayenne pepper
1 Tbsp. chopped fresh parsley *or* cilantro

Prick eggplant in several places with a fork. Place on a baking sheet and broil for about 20 minutes, turning several times so that skin chars on all sides. Let cool, then cut in half and scrape flesh into a bowl. Discard skin. Mash eggplant with remaining ingredients. Cover and chill before serving. Sprinkle with additional parsley for a garnish.

Serve with whole wheat pita bread wedges.

Variations:

•Eliminate tahini and lemon juice. Substitute 1/4 cup red wine vinegar and 1 to 2 Tbsp. olive oil.

•Eliminate tahini and cumin. Add 1/4 cup plain non-fat yogurt. Garnish with chopped parsley or paprika.

•Add 1 cup chopped tomatoes

•Add 1 tsp. oregano

Serves 12

Per serving:	Calories	Fat (g)	Cholesterol (mg)	Fiber (g)	Sodium (mg)
	37	2	0	2	46

Crab Stuffed Mushrooms

24 large mushrooms, stems removed
  and chopped
1 to 2 Tbsp. olive oil
1 to 1 1/2 cups flaked crab
4 egg whites

3 Tbsp. light, cholesterol-free mayonnaise
1/2 cup chopped onion
2 tsp. lemon juice
1/2 cup bread crumbs
1/4 cup Parmesan cheese

Clean mushroom caps. Brush each lightly with oil. Arrange on a non-stick baking sheet.

Combine chopped stems with remaining ingredients, except cheese. Fill mushroom caps and sprinkle lightly with cheese.

Bake at 375° for 15 to 20 minutes or until lightly browned.

Yield: 24; 1 serving = 1 mushroom

Per serving:	Calories	Fat (g)	Cholesterol (mg)	Fiber (g)	Sodium (mg)
	41	2	11	0	126

Marinated Mushrooms

1 1/2 lbs. small mushrooms, cleaned
1/2 onion, thinly sliced
1/2 cup lemon juice *or* red wine vinegar
1/4 cup water
2 Tbsp. olive oil
1 clove garlic, minced

2 Tbsp. minced fresh parsley
2 Tbsp. Dijon mustard
1 tsp. *each* oregano and tarragon
1/4 tsp. salt
Freshly ground pepper

Place mushrooms and onions in a shallow bowl. Combine remaining ingredients and mix thoroughly. Pour over mushrooms tossing gently to coat. Cover bowl and refrigerate overnight, stirring occasionally.

Variation: Add 2 cups lightly steamed broccoli florets or 1 pkg. frozen artichoke hearts, cooked and drained.

Yield: 8 appetizer servings

Per serving:	Calories	Fat (g)	Cholesterol (mg)	Fiber (g)	Sodium (mg)
	68	4	0	5	407

HealthMark "Gorp"

A high fiber munchie

Combine any or all of the following and munch with zest!

Plain popcorn (season with garlic, onion or chili powder)
Bran, Wheat, Corn or Rice Chex
Crispix cereal
Shredded Wheat with Bran squares
Raisins
Unsalted, dry roasted nuts (use sparingly)

Cold

Cold Peach 17
Gazpacho 17
Two Melon 18

Hot

Carrot Bisque 19
Creamy Potato 20
Fisherman's Stew 18
Garden Vegetable 22
Hearty Lentil 23
Minestrone 21
Mushroom Barley 20
Salmon Chowder 19
Senate Bean 22
Split Pea 23

Gazpacho

2 unpeeled cucumbers, seeded
5 tomatoes, cored
1 onion, white *or* red
1 green pepper, seeded

1 clove garlic, minced
1/4 cup *each* red wine vinegar and olive oil
1/4 tsp. *each* celery salt and cumin

Coarsely chop vegetables. Puree in blender or food processor. Blend in vinegar, oil, celery salt and cumin. Chill before serving.

Serves 6 to 8

Per serving:	Calories	Fat (g)	Cholesterol (mg)	Fiber (g)	Sodium (mg)
	92	7	0	1	55

Cold Peach Soup

1¹/2 lbs. ripe peaches, peeled,
  pitted and sliced
2 cups plain non-fat yogurt

1 cup orange juice
1 cup pineapple juice
1/4 cup dry Sherry (optional)

Puree peaches in blender or food processor until smooth. Add remaining ingredients and blend thoroughly. Chill before serving.

Serves 8

Variation: Substitute ripe, unpeeled nectarines for peaches or use a combination of peaches, nectarines and/or strawberries.

Per serving:	Calories	Fat (g)	Cholesterol (mg)	Fiber (g)	Sodium (mg)
	118	1	3	1	42

Two Melon Soup

(from The Denver Dry Tearoom)

1 small ripe cantaloupe
2 Tbsp. lemon juice
1/2 ripe honeydew

3 Tbsp. lime juice
2 tsp. chopped fresh mint

Peel, seed and coarsely chop melons. In a food processor or blender puree cantaloupe with lemon juice in batches until smooth. Repeat with honeydew, lime juice and mint. Chill each in separate bowls.

To serve, pour at the **same** time (using two measuring cups) equal amounts of both soups into chilled bowls. Garnish with mint leaves.

Serves 6

Per serving:	Calories	Fat (g)	Cholesterol (mg)	Fiber (g)	Sodium (mg)
	34	0	0	1	13

Fisherman's Stew

1 Tbsp. olive oil
3 cloves garlic, minced
2 onions, chopped
2 carrots, chopped
2 stalks celery, chopped
1/4 tsp. crushed fennel seeds *or*
  1/8 tsp. crushed saffron threads
1 28-oz. can Italian tomatoes,
  chopped
1/2 cup dry white wine

1/2 tsp. crushed red pepper
1/2 tsp. thyme
1 bay leaf
1 8-oz. bottle clam juice
1 cup water
1 lb. fish filets (sole, flounder, orange
  roughy *or* halibut), cut into bite-sized
  pieces
1 Tbsp. anise-flavored apertif (such as
  Pernod or Ricard) (optional)

Saute garlic and onions in oil until soft. Add carrots, celery, fennel, tomatoes and juices, wine, pepper, thyme, bay leaf, clam juice and water. Bring to a boil, then simmer, covered, about 15 minutes or until vegetables are just tender. Add fish; cook about 4 to 5 minutes. Stir in apertif. Serve immediately.

Serves 4

Per serving:	Calories	Fat (g)	Cholesterol (mg)	Fiber (g)	Sodium (mg)
	374	13	58	4	326

Salmon Chowder

1 onion, chopped
2 unpeeled potatoes, diced
3 cups water
1/2 tsp. Lite Salt™

1 tsp. dill
1 16-oz. can salt-free whole kernel corn
1 16-oz. can salmon, drained and flaked
4 cups non-fat milk

Combine onion, potato, water, salt and dill in a medium saucepan. Bring to a boil, then reduce heat and simmer until potatoes are tender, 20 to 30 minutes.

Add corn and salmon; mix well. Stir in milk. Heat, but do not let chowder boil. Serve hot.

Serves 6

Per serving:	Calories	Fat (g)	Cholesterol (mg)	Fiber (g)	Sodium (mg)
	258	4	55	3	557

Carrot Bisque

3 cups diced carrots
1 onion, chopped
2 cups water
1 tsp. chicken bouillon granules

1 shallot, quartered
1 tsp. tarragon
1 bay leaf
1/4 tsp. nutmeg

Combine carrots with remaining ingredients. Cook, covered, over medium heat until carrots are tender, 15 to 20 minutes. Discard by leaf. Puree carrot mixture in blender or food processor until smooth. Serve warm or chilled. Garnish with chopped chives.

Variation: For Zucchini Bisque, substitute zucchini for carrots, omitting nutmeg.

Yield: 4 1/2 cups; serves 4 to 5

Per serving:	Calories	Fat (g)	Cholesterol (mg)	Fiber (g)	Sodium (mg)
	42	3	3	2	234

Creamy Potato Soup

1 Tbsp. olive oil
1 onion, thinly sliced
1/4 tsp. *each* oregano and basil
1/2 tsp. thyme
4 unpeeled potatoes, diced

2 cups salt-free chicken broth, defatted
2 cups water
1 cup low-fat buttermilk *or* evaporated non-fat milk
1/2 tsp. Lite Salt™
Black pepper to taste

In a 2 quart pan saute onion and herbs in olive oil until tender. Add potatoes, broth and water; cover and simmer 20 to 30 minutes or until potatoes are tender. Stir in buttermilk, salt and pepper.

Serves 4 to 6

Per serving:	Calories	Fat (g)	Cholesterol (mg)	Fiber (g)	Sodium (mg)
	112	3	1	1	141

Mushroom Barley Soup

1/2 lb. mushrooms, sliced
1/2 cup diced onion
1 clove garlic, minced
1 Tbsp. liquid margarine *or* olive oil
1/4 cup whole wheat flour
5 cups salt-free chicken broth, defatted

1/2 cup barley
2 Tbsp. dry sherry (optional)
1 Tbsp. Worcestershire sauce
1 Tbsp. low-sodium soy sauce
1/4 cup chopped fresh parsley
1 tsp. thyme

In a large saucepan, saute mushrooms, onion and garlic in margarine until onion is soft. With a slotted spoon, remove vegetables from pan. Sprinkle in flour and cook over medium heat until flour is lightly browned. Gradually stir in broth, then add barley, sherry, Worcestershire, soy, parsley and thyme.

Bring to a boil, then cover and simmer for 45 minutes, stirring occasionally. Add mushroom mixture and continue simmering 15 to 20 minutes longer or until barley is tender.

Serves 4 to 6

Per serving:	Calories	Fat (g)	Cholesterol (mg)	Fiber (g)	Sodium (mg)
	90	3	0	4	165

Minestrone

1 cup Great Northern beans, uncooked
1 Tbsp. olive oil
1 large onion, chopped
1 leek, washed well and sliced
2 to 3 cloves garlic, minced
1/4 cup chopped fresh parsley
1 tsp. *each* basil, oregano and thyme
1 cup sliced celery, including tops
1 green *or* red bell pepper, chopped

1 cup sliced carrots
1 cup green beans, cut into 1" pieces
1 28-oz. can Italian tomatoes, chopped
1 cup zucchini, sliced
1 tsp. Lite Salt™
1 cup uncooked small pasta (eggless)
 (e.g. small macaroni shells)
1 10-oz. pkg. frozen peas, thawed

Soak beans according to directions on page 98. Discard soaking water and add 6 cups fresh water. Saute onion, leek and garlic in olive oil. Add to beans along with parsley, basil, oregano and thyme. Bring to a boil, then simmer, covered, 1 to 2 hours or until beans are tender stirring occasionally.

Add remaining vegetables, salt and pasta. Continue to simmer until tender, about 30 minutes.

Put 1/4 cup peas in each soup bowl then add hot soup. Sprinkle with 1 Tbsp. Parmesan cheese if desired.

Serves 6 to 8

Per serving:	Calories	Fat (g)	Cholesterol (mg)	Fiber (g)	Sodium (mg)
	166	2	0	7	450

Garden Vegetable Soup

2 tsp. olive oil
1 onion, chopped
1/2 cup diced celery
1 clove garlic, minced
1 28-oz. can Italian tomatoes
5 cups water
1 cup *each* sliced zucchini,
   sliced carrots and cut green beans

1/2 cup *each* chopped green and red bell
   pepper
1/2 cup eggless macaroni, uncooked
2 Tbsp. chopped fresh parsley
1 tsp. basil
1/2 tsp Lite Salt™

Heat oil in 4 quart saucepan. Saute onion, celery and garlic until tender. Add water and beans; bring to a boil. Cook, covered, over medium heat until beans are tender, 20 to 30 minutes.

Add tomatoes and vegetables. Cook, covered, until vegetables are tender, about 15 minutes. Stir in macaroni, parsley and basil. Cook, stirring occasionally, until macaroni is al dente, about 8 to 10 minutes.

Yield: 6 cups; 1 serving = 1 1/2 cups

Per serving:	Calories	Fat (g)	Cholesterol (mg)	Fiber (g)	Sodium (mg)
	153	3	0	5	311

Senate Bean Soup

2 cups Great Northern beans (*or* other
   white bean), uncooked
1/4 tsp. black pepper
1 bay leaf
1 to 2 tsp. liquid smoke
1 clove garlic, minced

2 cups chopped celery
1 cup *each* chopped carrots and
   chopped onions
1 cup salt-free tomatoes, pureed
1/4 cup chopped parsley
1/2 tsp. Lite Salt™

In a large pot soak beans overnight in 4 to 6 cups water. Drain and add 6 cups fresh water, pepper, bay leaf, liquid smoke and garlic. Bring to a boil, skimming as necessary. Simmer for 2 hours or until beans are tender.

Remove 1 to 2 cups beans and puree or mash until smooth. Return to pan. Add remaining ingredients and simmer, partially covered, an additional 1 to 1 1/2 hours or until thickened.

Serves 6

Per serving:	Calories	Fat (g)	Cholesterol (mg)	Fiber (g)	Sodium (mg)
	268	1	0	22	92

Split Pea Soup

1 Tbsp. olive oil
1 onion, chopped
2 to 3 cloves garlic, minced
1 unpeeled potato, diced
2 cups sliced carrots
6 cups salt-free chicken broth,
  defatted *or* water

3 cups dried split peas
1 bay leaf
1/2 tsp. *each* thyme and marjoram
1 tsp. liquid smoke *or* 1/2 tsp. salt (optional)
1/2 tsp. Lite Salt™

Saute onions and garlic in olive oil until soft. Add remaining ingredients. Bring to a boil, then simmer, covered, until peas are soft, 1 to 1 1/2 hours. Stir occasionally. Remove bay leaf before serving.

Serves 4 to 6

Per serving:	Calories	Fat (g)	Cholesterol (mg)	Fiber (g)	Sodium (mg)
	421	4	0	5	132

Hearty Lentil Soup

1 1/2 cups lentils
1 Tbsp. olive oil
1 onion, chopped
1 clove garlic, minced
2 cups salt-free chicken *or* beef
  broth, defatted
4 cups water

1 cup *each* sliced carrots and celery
1 cup chopped cabbage
1 unpeeled potato, diced
1 tsp. liquid smoke
1/2 tsp. *each* thyme and marjoram
Black pepper to taste

Wash and drain lentils. In a 4 quart pan saute onion and garlic in olive oil until soft. Add lentils and remaining ingredients. Bring to a boil. Skim if necessary. Reduce heat and simmer, covered, for 45 to 60 minutes until lentils and vegetables are tender. Stir occasionally. Remove bay leaf before serving.

Yield: about 2 quarts; 1 serving = 1 cup

Per serving:	Calories	Fat (g)	Cholesterol (mg)	Fiber (g)	Sodium (mg)
	174	2	0	3	36

Salads and Dressings

Cooking for a Healthier Ever After

Seasoning Mixes

To prepare Seasoning Mixes, combine all ingredients in a small jar and mix well. Store tightly covered. Use in place of salt to enhance the flavor of foods.

Spicy Seasoning Mix

2 tsp. *each* onion powder and basil
1 tsp. *each* dry mustard and paprika
1/2 tsp. *each* garlic powder, thyme,
    celery seed, parsley, savory, marjoram
    and curry powder
1/4 tsp. black *or* cayenne pepper

Yield: 1/2 cup

Savory Seasoning Mix

1 1/4 tsp. celery seed
2 Tbsp. marjoram
2 Tbsp. savory

2 Tbsp. thyme
1 Tbsp. basil

Use for salads, soups, fish and poultry.

Yield: 1/2 cup

Mexican Seasoning Mix

6 Tbsp. chili powder
2 Tbsp. cumin
1 1/2 tsp. *each* onion and garlic powder

Optional:
3/4 tsp. *each* thyme and oregano
1 Tbsp. basil
1/2 tsp. black pepper

For a Mexican flair sprinkle over salads or on chicken or fish before grilling.

Yield: 1/2 cup

Seafood Seasoning Mix

4 tsp. dried parsley
2 Tbsp. chives, dill *or*
   tarragon
1 1/2 tsp. black pepper
1/2 Tbsp. dried lemon zest

Optional:
1 1/2 tsp. dry mustard *or* garlic powder
1 tsp. minced fresh ginger

Use for poaching fish: add 2 teaspoons seasoning mixture to poaching liquid for each pound of fish.

Yield: 1/2 cup

Oriental Seasoning Mix

2 Tbsp. onion powder
2 Tbsp. garlic powder

2 Tbsp. minced fresh ginger
2 Tbsp. black pepper

Sprinkle on fish or poultry.

Yield: 1/2 cup

Vinaigrette Dressing

1/4 cup *each* red wine vinegar and water
3/4 cup olive oil
1/4 tsp. *each* salt and pepper
1/2 tsp. *each* paprika and
   dry mustard

1 clove garlic, minced
1 Tbsp. parsley
1/2 tsp. *each* basil and oregano

Whisk all ingredients together. Store in a tightly covered jar. Shake well before serving.

Yield: 1 1/4 cups; 1 serving = 2 Tbsp.

Per serving:	Calories	Fat (g)	Cholesterol (mg)	Fiber (g)	Sodium (mg)
	121	14	0	0	45

Ranch Dressing

1 pkg. Hidden Valley Ranch Dressing mix
Low-fat buttermilk
Plain non-fat yogurt

Prepare dressing according to package directions, substituting yogurt for mayonnaise. Use as a topping for baked potatoes, a dip for raw vegetables or use instead of mayonnaise in tuna or chicken salad.

Note: Ranch Dressing contains 165 mg. of sodium per tablespoon, less than other dressings, but it is still wise to use it sparingly.

1 serving = 2 Tbsp.

Per serving:	Calories	Fat (g)	Cholesterol (mg)	Fiber (g)	Sodium (mg)
	16	0	1	0	165

Bloomingdale's Salad Dressing

1/2 cup olive *or* safflower oil
1/2 cup red wine vinegar
1/4 cup Oriental sesame oil

Blend ingredients together and season with 1/4 to 1/2 tsp. of any or all of the following: black pepper, paprika, sugar or apple juice concentrate, celery seed, garlic, onion, basil, thyme, chervil, parsley, Worcestershire sauce, dry mustard.

Yield: 1 1/4 cups; 1 serving = 2 Tbsp.

Per serving:	Calories	Fat (g)	Cholesterol (mg)	Fiber (g)	Sodium (mg)
	155	17	0	0	3

Mustard Vinaigrette

1 1/2 tsp. Dijon mustard
2 Tbsp. lemon juice

6 Tbsp. olive oil
1/4 tsp. *each* salt and white pepper

Whisk all ingredients together.

Yield: 1/2 cup; 1 serving = 2 Tbsp.

Per serving:	Calories	Fat (g)	Cholesterol (mg)	Fiber (g)	Sodium (mg)
	183	20	0	0	158

Pommery Mustard Dressing

(from the Brown Palace Hotel)

1/2 cup Pommery mustard
1 egg white
6 Tbsp. red wine vinegar

1 Tbsp. honey
3/4 cup olive oil

Blend mustard, egg white, vinegar and honey in a blender or food processor. With motor running, pour in oil in a thin stream.

Yield: about 1 1/2 cups; 1 serving = 2 Tbsp.

Per serving:	Calories	Fat (g)	Cholesterol (mg)	Fiber (g)	Sodium (mg)
	135	14	0	0	134

Creamy Cucumber Dressing

1 unpeeled cucumber, seeded
1¹/2 cups 1% cottage cheese
¹/4 cup plain non-fat yogurt

¹/4 cup chopped onion *or*
  2 green onions, thinly sliced
1 tsp. dill

Combine all ingredients in blender or food processor. Puree until very smooth. Use as a salad dressing or as a sauce for salmon.

Yield: 1³/4 cups; 1 serving = 2 Tbsp.

Per serving:	Calories	Fat (g)	Cholesterol (mg)	Fiber (g)	Sodium (mg)
	23	0	1	0	102

Green Goddess Salad Dressing

(from Marina Landing)

1 cup fresh spinach, stemmed and
  torn into bite-sized pieces
¹/2 cup chopped fresh parsley
2 cups plain non-fat yogurt
1 Tbsp. honey
¹/2 tsp. garlic, minced

1 Tbsp. Dijon mustard
1 Tbsp. dill
1¹/2 tsp. basil
¹/2 tsp. thyme
¹/2 tsp. white pepper
2 Tbsp. olive oil

Place the spinach, parsley and 1 cup yogurt in a blender or a food processor. Puree until smooth, then add the remaining yogurt and blend again until smooth.

Add all of the other ingredients except the olive oil and blend. Then, with the blender or food processor running, pour in the oil in a thin, steady stream. Mix until the oil is completely incorporated into the salad dressing.

Yield: 2³/4 cups; 1 serving = 2 Tbsp.

Per serving:	Calories	Fat (g)	Cholesterol (mg)	Fiber (g)	Sodium (mg)
	30	2	1	0	26

Creamy Dill Dressing

1/4 cup olive oil
2 Tbsp. light, cholesterol-free mayonnaise
3 Tbsp. vinegar

1 Tbsp. Dijon mustard
1 tsp. dill

In a small bowl, whisk all ingredients together until well blended and thickened. Chill before using as a salad dressing or a dip. Also good as a marinade for fish: brush on both sides of fish and marinate for one hour before cooking.

Yield: about 1/2 cup; 1 serving = 2 Tbsp.

Per serving:	Calories	Fat (g)	Cholesterol (mg)	Fiber (g)	Sodium (mg)
	100	11	0	0	66

Honey Mustard Dressing

1 cup plain non-fat yogurt
1 Tbsp. honey

1 Tbsp. Dijon mustard
1/8 tsp. garlic powder

Combine ingredients and blend well. Chill before serving.

Yield: 1 cup; 1 serving = 2 Tbsp.

Per serving:	Calories	Fat (g)	Cholesterol (mg)	Fiber (g)	Sodium (mg)
	28	1	2	0	44

Orange Poppy Seed Dressing

Delicious on fruit salad

1 cup plain non-fat yogurt
1 Tbsp. honey, brown sugar *or*
   apple juice concentrate
1 Tbsp. frozen orange juice concentrate,
   thawed

1 tsp. poppy seed
1 tsp. orange zest

Combine ingredients and blend well. Chill before serving.

Yield: 1 cup; 1 serving = 2 Tbsp.

Per serving:	Calories	Fat (g)	Cholesterol (mg)	Fiber (g)	Sodium (mg)
	31	1	2	0	20

Poppy Seed Dressing

Nice on fresh fruit salad

1/3 cup honey
1/3 cup raspberry *or* white wine vinegar
1 tsp. orange *or* lemon zest

1/2 tsp. dry mustard
1 cup canola *or* safflower oil
2 Tbsp. poppy seeds

In a small bowl, whisk together honey, vinegar, zest and mustard. Gradually whisk in oil until all is incorporated. Stir in poppy seeds. (May also be prepared in blender or food processor.)

Yield: about 1 3/4 cups; 1 serving = 1 Tbsp.

Per serving:	Calories	Fat (g)	Cholesterol (mg)	Fiber (g)	Sodium (mg)
	123	8	0	0	0

Yogurt Mustard Sauce

1¹/2 cups plain non-fat yogurt
2 Tbsp. Dijon mustard

1 clove garlic, minced (optional)
1 tsp. soy sauce

Combine all ingredients and blend well. Cover and chill.

Use as a topping for baked potatoes, as a salad dressing or a dip for fresh vegetables.

Yield: 1¹/2 cups; 1 serving = 2 Tbsp.

Per serving:	Calories	Fat (g)	Cholesterol (mg)	Fiber (g)	Sodium (mg)
	21	1	2	0	90

HealthMark Mayonnaise

1 cup plain non-fat yogurt
¹/2 cup light, cholesterol-free mayonnaise

Combine yogurt and mayonnaise in a small bowl and mix well. Cover and store in refrigerator. Use for a sandwich spread or mix with tuna, turkey or chicken salad.

Variation: Add 1 to 2 tsp. Dijon mustard.

Yield: 1¹/2 cups; 1 serving = 1 Tbsp.

Per serving:	Calories	Fat (g)	Cholesterol (mg)	Fiber (g)	Sodium (mg)
	23	2	1	0	40

Zero Calorie Dressing

1/2 cup salt-free tomato juice
2 Tbsp. lemon juice *or* red wine vinegar
1 Tbsp. minced onion
1 tsp. parsley
1 clove garlic, minced

Combine all ingredients in a jar with a tightly fitting lid. Shake well before serving.

Variation: Add 1/2 tsp. of any of the following: basil, oregano, rosemary, savory, horseradish and/or dry mustard.

Yield: about 3/4 cup; 1 serving = 2 Tbsp.

Per serving:	Calories	Fat (g)	Cholesterol (mg)	Fiber (g)	Sodium (mg)
	7	0	0	0	2

Hot Potato Salad

3 to 4 new potatoes (unpeeled), scrubbed
2 garlic cloves, minced
1/3 cup chopped fresh parsley
1/4 tsp. celery seed
1 Tbsp. olive oil
4 Tbsp. Balsamic vinegar
1/4 tsp. Lite Salt™

Cut potatoes into quarters and steam until tender. Cool slightly and cube.

Meanwhile, chop garlic, parsley and celery seed in a food processor. Blend in oil, vinegar and salt. Mix dressing with hot potatoes and serve warm.

Serves 3 to 4

Per serving:	Calories	Fat (g)	Cholesterol (mg)	Fiber (g)	Sodium (mg)
	127	4	0	2	67

French Potato Salad

2 lbs. unpeeled new potatoes
4 Tbsp. low-sodium, defatted
   chicken broth
4 Tbsp. wine vinegar
1 tsp. dry mustard

Black pepper to taste
2 to 3 Tbsp. olive oil
1/2 cup thinly sliced green onions *or*
   chopped red onions
1/4 cup chopped fresh parsley

Steam potatoes for 20 to 30 minutes or until just tender. Cool, then slice. Place in a large mixing bowl. Add chicken broth and mix gently.

Blend together vinegar, mustard and pepper. Pour over warm potatoes and blend well. Let potatoes stand for 10 minutes, then stir in olive oil, onions and parsley.

Serve at room temperature.

Serves 6 to 8

Per serving:	Calories	Fat (g)	Cholesterol (mg)	Fiber (g)	Sodium (mg)
	118	4	0	1	4

Buttermilk Cole Slaw

Dressing:
2/3 cup low-fat buttermilk
1/2 cup plain non-fat yogurt
1/4 cup light, cholesterol-free mayonnaise
1 Tbsp. fresh lemon juice
2 tsp. lemon zest
2 tsp. dill
1 tsp. celery seed
1/4 tsp. Lite Salt™
1/2 cup thinly sliced green onions

Slaw:
1 head green cabbage, shredded
2 carrots, shredded
1/2 cup thinly sliced green onions

For dressing: In a small bowl, whisk together all ingredients, except green onions, until well blended. Add 1/2 cup green onions and mix well. Cover and refrigerate.

In a large bowl, toss together cabbage, carrots and remaining green onions. Add dressing and mix well. Serve immediately or cover and chill before serving.

Serves 8

Per serving:	Calories	Fat (g)	Cholesterol (mg)	Fiber (g)	Sodium (mg)
	44	3	1	0	118

Rainbow Cole Slaw

1 small head green cabbage,
  finely shredded
1 small head red cabbage, finely shredded
2 unpeeled Golden Delicious apples,
  cored and diced
4 carrots, shredded
2 green *or* red bell peppers, diced
1 red onion, thinly sliced

Dressing:
2/3 cup frozen orange juice concentrate,
  thawed
1/3 cup raspberry *or* red wine vinegar
2 tsp. dry mustard
1/2 tsp. minced fresh ginger
1 clove garlic, minced

In a large bowl combine shredded cabbage, apple, carrot, green pepper and onion.

In a small bowl, whisk together ingredients for dressing. Combine with cabbage mixture and toss to mix thoroughly. Cover and chill before serving.

Serves 10 to 12

Per serving:	Calories	Fat (g)	Cholesterol (mg)	Fiber (g)	Sodium (mg)
	79	1	0	4	30

Zucchini Apple Slaw

1/4 cup light, cholesterol-free mayonnaise
1/4 cup plain non-fat yogurt
2 Tbsp. cider vinegar
1 Tbsp. brown sugar *or* honey

1 tsp. caraway *or* poppy seed
4 cups shredded zucchini
6 green onions, thinly sliced
3 apples (unpeeled), cored and diced

In a small bowl, combine, mayonnaise, yogurt, vinegar, brown sugar and caraway seeds. Set aside while preparing salad.

In a large bowl, toss together zucchini, onion and diced apple. Add dressing and mix lightly until well coated. Cover and refrigerate 2 to 4 hours before serving.

Serves 6 to 8

Per serving:	Calories	Fat (g)	Cholesterol (mg)	Fiber (g)	Sodium (mg)
	86	3	0	2	57

Waldorf Salad

2 cups diced unpeeled apples
1 cup diced celery
1/4 cup raisins *or* seedless grapes, halved

1/2 cup plain, non-fat yogurt mixed with
  1 to 2 Tbsp. orange juice concentrate
2 Tbsp. chopped walnuts

Mix all ingredients together; chill. Serve sprinkled with walnuts.

Serves 4

Per serving:	Calories	Fat (g)	Cholesterol (mg)	Fiber (g)	Sodium (mg)
	98	1	2	3	54

Garden Cottage Cheese Salad

1 1/2 cups 1% cottage cheese
1/2 cup unpeeled cucumber,
  seeded and chopped
1/4 cup *each* chopped green pepper
  and grated carrot
1 green onion, thinly sliced

1 Tbsp. minced fresh parsley
2 Tbsp. chopped ripe olives (rinse
  and drain before chopping)
1/2 tsp. Dijon mustard
1/8 tsp. *each* white pepper and
  Worcestershire sauce

In a medium bowl combine all ingredients and blend well. Serve on lettuce-lined plates.

Serves 4

Per serving:	Calories	Fat (g)	Cholesterol (mg)	Fiber (g)	Sodium (mg)
	76	2	4	1	477

Marinated Vegetable Salad

Assorted fresh vegetables to total 4 to 5 cups:

Broccoli, steamed until just tender	Zucchini
Cauliflower, steamed until just tender	Jicama
Carrots	Cherry tomatoes, halved
Green beans	Red, white or green onion
Celery	1/3 to 1/2 cup Vinaigrette Dressing
Mushrooms	(page 59)

Chop or slice vegetables into bite-size pieces. In a large bowl combine vegetables with dressing; toss to coat evenly. Cover and refrigerate overnight. Serve chilled.

Variation: Add 2 cups cooked eggless pasta and/or 1 cup cooked, dried beans (e.g. kidney or garbanzo).

Serves 4 to 6

Per serving:	Calories	Fat (g)	Cholesterol (mg)	Fiber (g)	Sodium (mg)
	139	11	0	3	17

Red and Orange Salad

4 to 5 carrots, sliced	1 Tbsp. brown sugar *or*
1 red bell pepper, cored and seeded	apple juice concentrate
1 green pepper, cored and seeded	1 tsp. ground coriander
1/2 red onion	1 to 2 Tbsp. chopped fresh parsley
1/2 cup vinegar	

Steam carrots until just tender, about 3 minutes. Rinse under cold water and drain thoroughly. Transfer to a large bowl. Thinly slice peppers and onions; mix with vinegar, sugar, coriander, parsley and carrots. Cover and chill several hours or overnight to blend flavors. Serve at room temperature.

Serves 4

Per serving:	Calories	Fat (g)	Cholesterol (mg)	Fiber (g)	Sodium (mg)
	67	0	0	2	48

Sweet and Sour Zucchini

1 Tbsp. chopped onion *or*
  1/4 cup sliced green onion
1/2 cup sugar or apple juice concentrate
1 tsp. black pepper
1/2 tsp. dill
1/3 cup olive *or* safflower oil

2/3 cup cider *or* white vinegar
1/2 cup white wine vinegar
8 cups thinly sliced zucchini
1/2 cup chopped green pepper
1/2 cup chopped celery

Mix together onion, sugar, pepper, dill, oil and vinegars. Combine with vegetables. Cover. Chill several hours or overnight. Drain well before serving.

Serves 16

Per serving:	Calories	Fat (g)	Cholesterol (mg)	Fiber (g)	Sodium (mg)
	85	2	0	1	6

Marinated Cucumbers

2 unpeeled cucumbers
3/4 cup white vinegar
1/4 cup sugar *or* apple juice concentrate

3 green onions, thinly sliced
1/2 tsp. dill

Score cucumbers with a fork; remove seeds and slice thinly. Mix vinegar and sugar in a saucepan. Bring to a boil to allow sugar to dissolve. Cool. Mix with cucumber, green onion and dill. Marinate several hours or overnight.

Serves 4 to 6

Per serving:	Calories	Fat (g)	Cholesterol (mg)	Fiber (g)	Sodium (mg)
	42	0	0	0	3

Creamy Cucumbers

1¹/2 cups plain non-fat yogurt
2 cucumbers, seeded
2 cloves garlic, minced

2 tsp. olive oil
1 tsp. dill

Place yogurt in a strainer lined with cheesecloth or 3 coffee filters. Let drain for 1¹/2 to 2 hours. Discard liquid (yogurt will be thicker).

Meanwhile, thinly slice cucumbers. Mix with garlic, olive oil, dill and yogurt. Cover and chill 1 hour before serving.

Serves 4

Per serving:	Calories	Fat (g)	Cholesterol (mg)	Fiber (g)	Sodium (mg)
	86	4	5	0	64

Mushroom Celery Salad

3 Tbsp. *each* red wine vinegar and water
1/2 tsp. Worcestershire sauce
1/4 tsp. garlic, minced
1/4 tsp. Lite Salt™
Black pepper to taste

1/4 cup olive oil
1/2 lb. mushrooms, thinly sliced
1¹/2 cups celery, thinly sliced
1/2 cup thinly sliced red bell pepper

For dressing: blend vinegar, Worcestershire sauce, garlic, salt and pepper in a blender or food processor. With motor running, add oil in a thin stream.

Combine mushrooms, celery and red bell pepper in a large bowl. Add dressing and toss well. Serve chilled or at room temperature.

Serves 8

Per serving:	Calories	Fat (g)	Cholesterol (mg)	Fiber (g)	Sodium (mg)
	74	7	0	2	98

Hunan Eggplant Salad

1 medium eggplant
1 Tbsp. olive *or* safflower oil
1 cup water
1/4 cup low-sodium soy sauce
6 thin slices fresh ginger
2 cloves garlic, minced

1 tsp. brown sugar *or* apple juice concentrate
3 Tbsp. red wine vinegar
1/3 cup coarsely chopped fresh cilantro
2 tsp. minced fresh ginger
1/4 to 1/2 tsp. dried hot red chiles

Remove stem from eggplant. Cut lengthwise into 1/2" thick slices. Brush lightly with oil. Place on a baking sheet and bake at 350° for 10 to 15 minutes, or until soft. Cool, then chop into 1/2" pieces.

Combine eggplant, water, soy, ginger slices, garlic and brown sugar in a saucepan. Cover and simmer over low heat until eggplant mashes easily when pressed, about 20 to 30 minutes. Add vinegar. Cool, stirring occasionally.

Transfer to a serving dish, then sprinkle with cilantro, minced ginger and chiles. Serve at room temperature or chilled.

Serves 4 to 6

Per serving:	Calories	Fat (g)	Cholesterol (mg)	Fiber (g)	Sodium (mg)
	50	3	0	2	403

Alaskan Cobb Salad

6 oz. canned salmon
2 cups *each* Romaine and Iceberg
   lettuce, torn into bite-size pieces
2 green onions, thinly sliced

1 tomato, cored and diced
1/2 avocado, peeled and diced
Dijon Dressing (recipe follows)

Drain and flake salmon, reserving 2 Tbsp. liquid for the dressing. Toss lettuces together and arrange on a platter. Arrange onions, tomato, avocado and salmon in rows on top of lettuce. Serve with Dijon Dressing.

Dijon Dressing:
2 Tbsp. *each* olive oil and vinegar
2 Tbsp. reserved salmon liquid
1 Tbsp. chopped fresh parsley

1 tsp. Dijon mustard
3/4 tsp. lemon zest
1/4 tsp. thyme

Combine all ingredients, blending well.

Serves 2

Per serving:	Calories	Fat (g)	Cholesterol (mg)	Fiber (g)	Sodium (mg)
	374	28	58	4	378

Spinach Chutney Salad

Salad:
8 cups fresh spinach
1 apple, cored and cubed (unpeeled)
1/2 cup toasted walnuts *or* peanuts
1/2 cup golden raisins
6 green onions, thinly sliced

Dressing:
1/2 cup red wine vinegar
2/3 cup olive oil
1/4 cup chutney
1 tsp. curry powder
1 tsp. dry mustard
1/2 tsp. celery seed
1/4 tsp. minced fresh ginger

Tear spinach into bite-size pieces and place in a large bowl. Add chopped apple, nuts, raisi and green onion. Toss well and refrigerate while making dressing.

Dressing: in a small bowl, combine dressing ingredients and whisk until well blended. Ad just enough dressing to coat leaves and toss salad well.

Variation: Add cooked, cubed chicken or turkey (skinless).

Serves 8

Per serving:	Calories	Fat (g)	Cholesterol (mg)	Fiber (g)	Sodium (mg)
	273	23	0	3	41

Curried Chicken Salad

2 cups brown rice
4 cups water
1 tsp. curry powder
2 chicken breasts, skinned
1 8 oz. can water chestnuts, sliced
1 cup sliced celery

4 green onions, thinly sliced
1 cup green *or* red seedless grapes, halved
1/4 cup toasted pecans (optional)
Chutney dressing (recipe follows)
Fresh fruit for garnish

Combine rice, water and curry powder in a medium saucepan. Bring to a boil. Reduce heat, cover and simmer until tender, 45 to 50 minutes. Set aside to cool.

Meanwhile, bake chicken breasts in an 8" x 8" pan coated with cooking spray for 25 to 35 minutes or until done. Cool, then remove meat and dice.

In a medium bowl, combine rice, chicken, water chestnuts, green onion, celery, grapes and pecans. Mix well. Add 1/2 to 3/4 cup Chutney Dressing and toss to combine. Cover and refrigerate for 2 to 3 hours before serving. Garnish with fresh fruit.

Serves 4

Per serving:	Calories	Fat (g)	Cholesterol (mg)	Fiber (g)	Sodium (mg)
	531	21	50	5	691

Chutney Dressing

3 cloves garlic, minced
1 Tbsp. minced fresh ginger *or*
  1 tsp. powdered ginger
1 1/2 Tbsp. coarsely ground mustard

1/2 cup chutney
1/2 cup raspberry *or* red wine vinegar
3/4 cup olive *or* safflower oil

In a food processor or blender, puree garlic, ginger, mustard, chutney and vinegar. With the motor running, pour in oil in a thin stream. Cover and refrigerate before serving.

Yield: 2 cups; 1 serving = 2 Tbsp.

Per serving:	Calories	Fat (g)	Cholesterol (mg)	Fiber (g)	Sodium (mg)
	104	10	0	0	19

Oriental Chicken Salad

Dressing:
3 Tbsp. rice vinegar
1 Tbsp. Oriental sesame oil
3 drops of hot pepper sauce
1/4 tsp. Lite Salt™

Salad:
2 cups skinless chicken, cooked and
    shredded

5 cups shredded Romaine lettuce
1 cup snow peas, sliced
1 cup bean sprouts
1 8-oz. can water chestnuts,
    drained and sliced
1 carrot, julienne
1/4 cup chopped fresh cilantro
3 green onions, thinly sliced
1 Tbsp. sesame seeds, toasted

Combine dressing ingredients. Add 2 Tbsp. dressing to chicken and toss to coat well. Cover chicken and remaining dressing; refrigerate overnight.

Combine remaining ingredients in large bowl. Add marinated chicken and dressing; toss to combine. May be served chilled or at room temperature.

Serves 6 to 8

Per serving:	Calories	Fat (g)	Cholesterol (mg)	Fiber (g)	Sodium (mg)
	180	5	50	2	150

Turkey Apricot Salad

Honey-Mustard Dressing:
2 tsp. poppy seeds
2 Tbsp. honey
2 Tbsp. Dijon mustard
1/2 tsp. lemon zest
1/3 cup lemon juice
1/4 cup olive *or* safflower oil

Salad:
1/2 cup dried apricots, quartered
4 cups skinless, cubed, cooked turkey
1 red unpeeled apple, chopped
1 cup chopped celery
1/4 cup sliced green onions
Avocado (optional)

Combine dressing ingredients and blend well. In a large bowl marinate apricots in dressing for 30 minutes to soften. Add turkey, apple, celery and onion; mix well.

Serve on a plate lined with a lettuce leaf; garnish with fresh fruit and 1 or 2 slices of avocado per person.

Serves 6

Per serving:	Calories	Fat (g)	Cholesterol (mg)	Fiber (g)	Sodium (mg)
	315	14	71	2	167

Chicken Pasta Salad Primavera

Dressing:
1 cup olive *or* safflower oil
2/3 cup red wine vinegar
1 tsp. sugar *or* apple juice concentrate
1 clove garlic, minced
1/2 tsp. *each* salt and pepper
1 tsp. Dijon mustard
1 tsp. Worcestershire sauce
1 tsp. paprika

Salad:
1/2 lb. eggless pasta (e.g. bow ties),
   cooked and drained

2 cups cubed, cooked, skinless chicken
1/4 lb. fresh mushrooms, sliced
2 cups broccoli, cooked and chopped
1 10-oz. package frozen peas, thawed
1/2 pint cherry tomatoes, sliced in half
1 cup chopped celery
1/4 cup green onions, thinly sliced
1 8-oz. can water chestnuts, sliced
   (optional)
2 Tbsp. dried basil
1/2 tsp. black pepper

Mix together the ingredients for the dressing. Pour 1/3 cup of dressing over cooked pasta while it is still warm. Chill for at least 3 hours or overnight.

Add the chicken, vegetables, basil, pepper and 1/3 cup of dressing to the pasta and toss. Serve on lettuce lined plates. Serve remaining dressing on the side.

Serves 6 to 8

Variation: Substitute seafood (such as scallops, crab and/or salmon) for chicken.

Per serving:	Calories	Fat (g)	Cholesterol (mg)	Fiber (g)	Sodium (mg)
	247	4	32	4	110

Spinach Pasta Salad

8 oz. eggless tri-color fusilli pasta
4 cups fresh spinach, washed and stemmed
1 red onion, thinly sliced
1/2 cup Poppy Seed Dressing (page 63)

Cook pasta according to package directions, omitting salt. Drain well then toss with spinach leaves. When cool mix in onion slices and dressing. Add additional dressing as needed.

Serves 6 to 8

Per serving:	Calories	Fat (g)	Cholesterol (mg)	Fiber (g)	Sodium (mg)
	119	1	0	1	23

Sunflower Pasta Salad

4 oz. bow tie *or* other eggless pasta,
  cooked and drained
6 to 8 cherry tomatoes, halved
1/2 medium cucumber, thinly sliced
1/4 cup sliced black olives (rinse and
  drain before slicing)

4 radishes, thinly sliced
1/4 cup dry roasted, unsalted sunflower seeds
1/4 cup Vinaigrette Dressing (page 59)

Combine all ingredients, blending well. Cover and chill several hours before serving. May be served chilled or at room temperature.

Serves 2 to 3

Per serving:	Calories	Fat (g)	Cholesterol (mg)	Fiber (g)	Sodium (mg)
	331	20	3	2	111

Pink and Green Pasta Salad

Salad:
8 oz. eggless pasta (e.g. Rotini)
1/2 lb. cooked baby shrimp
1 10-oz. pkg. frozen peas,
   thawed and drained
4 green onions, thinly sliced
1 cup sliced celery, tops included
1/2 cup dry roasted, unsalted cashews

Dressing:
1 cup plain non-fat yogurt
1 to 2 Tbsp. light, cholesterol
   free mayonnaise
1 Tbsp. lemon juice
1 tsp. dill

Cook pasta according to package directions, omitting salt. Drain and cool to room temperature. Mix with shrimp, peas, vegetables and nuts.

Blend together dressing ingredients and toss with pasta mixture. Chill before serving.

Serves 4

Per serving:	Calories	Fat (g)	Cholesterol (mg)	Fiber (g)	Sodium (mg)
	530	17	83	5	408

Lemony Seafood Salad

1/4 cup rice vinegar
3 Tbsp. lemon juice
2 Tbsp. minced fresh ginger
1 1/2 Tbsp. honey
1 Tbsp. low-sodium soy sauce
Dash Tabasco sauce
1 lb. scallops

1/2 lb. shrimp, peeled and deveined
12 oz. eggless linguine *or* spaghetti
1 10-oz. pkg frozen peas,
  thawed and drained
1 Tbsp. Oriental sesame oil
6 green onions, thinly sliced
1 Tbsp. lemon zest

In a 3 to 4 quart pan, combine vinegar, lemon juice, ginger, honey, soy sauce, Tabasco, scallops and shrimp. Bring to a boil, stirring occasionally, then remove from heat. Cover and let stand until seafood is done, about 5 minutes; stir occasionally. Remove shrimp and scallops; refrigerate. Boil cooking liquid until reduced by half.

Meanwhile, cook pasta according to package directions, omitting salt. Pour into a colander and rinse with cold water until pasta is cool. Drain well.

In a large bowl, combine pasta, scallops, shrimp, peas, green onions, sesame oil, lemon zest and reduced cooking liquid. Toss to coat well. Serve, or cover and chill several hours before serving.

Serves: 4 to 6

Per serving:	Calories	Fat (g)	Cholesterol (mg)	Fiber (g)	Sodium (mg)
	406	5	95	2	469

Oriental Noodle Salad

Dressing:
1/4 cup olive *or* safflower oil
1/4 cup rice vinegar
2 Tbsp. low-sodium soy sauce
2 tsp. sugar *or* honey
1 tsp. dry mustard
1 tsp. natural-style peanut butter
1 tsp. Oriental sesame oil
1 tsp. minced fresh ginger

Salad:
10 dried Chinese mushrooms
12 oz. Oriental dried noodles (e.g. Soba),
  cooked and drained
1/4 lb. fresh snow peas, julienne
1 red bell pepper, seeded and julienne
1 medium jicama, peeled and julienne
4 carrots, sliced
1/4 cup toasted sesame seeds

Combine dressing ingredients and mix thoroughly. Set aside.

Soak mushrooms in hot water for 30 minutes or until softened. Drain and slice thinly, discarding tough stems. Combine with remaining ingredients. Add dressing and toss to blend thoroughly. Serve chilled or at room temperature.

Serves 4 to 6

Per serving:	Calories	Fat (g)	Cholesterol (mg)	Fiber (g)	Sodium (mg)
	380	15	0	2	253

Brown Rice Salad

Salad:
3 cups cooked brown rice
2 red bell peppers, seeded and chopped
3 green onions, thinly sliced
1 10-oz. pkg. frozen peas,
    thawed and drained
2 carrots, shredded *or* sliced
1/4 cup chopped fresh parsley
1/2 cup raisins *or* currants (optional)
1/4 cup chopped walnuts (optional)

Dressing:
1/3 cup apple cider vinegar
2 Tbsp. olive oil
1/2 tsp. *each* oregano and dry mustard
Dash cayenne

Combine salad ingredients in a medium bowl. In a small bowl, whisk together dressing ingredients.

Toss dressing with salad, blending thoroughly. Serve chilled or at room temperature.

Serves 4 to 6

Per serving:	Calories	Fat (g)	Cholesterol (mg)	Fiber (g)	Sodium (mg)
	236	4	0	6	350

Salmon Rice Salad

2 cups cooked brown rice
1/2 cup Vinaigrette Dressing (page 59)
1 7-oz. can salmon, rinsed,
    drained and flaked

1 cup chopped celery, tops included
1 cup frozen peas, thawed
1 cup asparagus, steamed until
    tender-crisp and cut into 1" pieces

Combine warm rice with dressing. Let stand until cool. Mix in remaining ingredients. Garnish with tomato wedges to serve.

Serves 4 to 6

Per serving:	Calories	Fat (g)	Cholesterol (mg)	Fiber (g)	Sodium (mg)
	253	13	23	3	400

Indonesian Rice Salad

(from Alfalfa's Market)

Salad:
1/4 lb. snow peas
2 cups cooked brown rice
2 to 3 green onions, thinly sliced
1 cup chopped celery
1/2 cup chopped fresh parsley
1 cup chopped green pepper
1 8-oz. can water chestnuts, sliced
1/4 lb. bean sprouts, washed and drained
1 cup diced pineapple (if canned,
   use juice pack)
1 unpeeled apple, seeded and chopped

1 cup halved red *or* green grapes
1/2 cup unsalted cashews
1/2 cup raisins
1/4 cup toasted sesame seeds

Dressing:
1/2 cup orange juice concentrate, thawed
1/4 cup olive *or* safflower oil
1 tsp. *each* minced fresh ginger
1 tsp. orange zest
2 tsp. tamari
1 clove garlic, minced

Steam snow peas for 2 to 3 minutes. Rinse under cold water, then drain well. In a large bowl combine with remaining ingredients and mix well.

Prepare dressing: blend together orange juice concentrate, oil, ginger, zest, tamari and garlic. Pour over salad and toss gently, blending well.

Serves 10 to 12

Per serving:	Calories	Fat (g)	Cholesterol (mg)	Fiber (g)	Sodium (mg)
	239	11	0	4	177

Breads

Miscellaneous

Muffins

Apricot-Prune Bran Muffins

A food processor makes quick work of these tasty muffins

1 1/2 cups All-Bran cereal (or other
   similar bran cereal)
1/2 cup *each* dried prunes and apricots
1 cup whole wheat flour
2 tsp. baking powder
1/2 tsp. baking soda

1/4 cup brown sugar
3/4 cup low-fat buttermilk
1/4 cup canola *or* safflower oil
4 egg whites
1 tsp. vanilla

Fit metal blade into work bowl of food processor. Add cereal, prunes and apricots. Process for 1 minute or until fruit is diced. Add remaining ingredients. Pulse three times, scrape down sides of workbowl, pulse three more times.

Spoon about 1/4 cup batter into each of 12 muffin cups coated with cooking spray. Bake at 375° for 20 to 25 minutes, until golden.

Yield: 12 muffins

Per serving:	Calories	Fat (g)	Cholesterol (mg)	Fiber (g)	Sodium (mg)
	195	5	0	6	259

Bran Muffins

2 cups bran cereal
1 cup non-fat milk
2 egg whites
1/4 cup canola *or* safflower oil

1 cup whole wheat flour
1/4 cup brown sugar
2 tsp. baking powder
1/2 cup raisins

Soak cereal in non-fat milk for 1 to 2 minutes to soften. Mix in egg whites and oil. Sift together flour, sugar and baking powder in a mixing bowl. Make a well in the center. Add the cereal mixture and raisins. Stir just until flour mixture is moistened. (Do not over mix or muffins will be tough.)

Spoon batter into muffin cups coated with cooking spray, filling 3/4 full. Bake at 425° for 20 to 25 minutes or until golden brown.

Variations:

• Add 1/2 cup chopped dried apricots, prunes or blueberries to dry ingredients.

• Eliminate bran cereal. Soak 1 cup rolled oats in 1 cup non-fat milk for 15 minutes. Blend with egg whites and oil; add to dry ingredients.

Yield: 10 to 12 muffins

Per serving:	Calories	Fat (g)	Cholesterol (mg)	Fiber (g)	Sodium (mg)
	152	5	0	5	242

Oat Bran Muffins

2 1/2 cups oat bran
1/3 cup brown sugar *or* 1/3 cup honey
2 tsp. baking powder
1 tsp. *each* cinnamon and orange zest
1/2 tsp. nutmeg
1/2 cup raisins

1 cup non-fat milk *or* orange juice
3 egg whites
1/4 cup canola *or* safflower oil
2 tsp. vanilla
1/2 cup unsweetened applesauce *or*
   2 bananas, mashed

Combine dry ingredients and raisins. Add milk, egg whites, oil, vanilla and applesauce. Mix just until moist.

Spoon batter into 12 muffin cups coated with cooking spray. Bake at 425° for 17 to 20 minutes.

Yield: 12 muffins

Per serving:	Calories	Fat (g)	Cholesterol (mg)	Fiber (g)	Sodium (mg)
	168	6	0	4	94

Carrot Sesame Muffins

1 1/2 cups whole wheat flour
1/2 cup wheat germ *or* oat bran
1/2 cup bran cereal (e.g. All-Bran)
2 Tbsp. sesame seeds
1 tsp. baking soda
2 tsp. cinnamon
1 tsp. nutmeg
1/2 tsp. allspice

1/4 tsp. cloves
2/3 cup orange juice
1/2 cup honey
1/3 cup canola *or* safflower oil
1/4 cup plain non-fat yogurt
3 carrots, peeled and grated
   (1 1/2 cups packed)

Mix together first 9 ingredients. In a large bowl whisk together orange juice, honey, oil and yogurt. Add flour mixture, stirring until just moistened. Mix in carrots.

Spoon into muffin cups coated with cooking spray, filling each 2/3 full. Bake at 350° for 25 to 30 minutes.

Yield: 18 muffins

Per serving:	Calories	Fat (g)	Cholesterol (mg)	Fiber (g)	Sodium (mg)
	139	5	1	2	87

Cinnamon Oat Muffins

1 3/4 cups non-fat milk
1 cup oat bran
1 cup rolled oats
2 egg whites
1/2 cup brown sugar
2 tsp. cinnamon

1/2 tsp. allspice
1/4 cup canola *or* safflower oil
1/2 cup *each* unbleached and
    whole wheat flour
2 tsp. baking powder
1/2 cup raisins

In a medium bowl combine milk, oat bran and oatmeal. Add egg whites, brown sugar, cinnamon, allspice and oil. Add combined flours and baking powder, mixing just until blended. Stir in raisins.

Divide batter among 15 muffin cups coated with cooking spray. Bake at 400° for 20 to 25 minutes, until golden.

Yield: 15 muffins

Per serving:	Calories	Fat (g)	Cholesterol (mg)	Fiber (g)	Sodium (mg)
	153	5	1	3	79

Honey Apple Muffins

1/4 cup canola *or* safflower oil
1/2 cup honey
2 egg whites
1 tsp. vanilla
1 cup whole wheat flour
1 tsp. baking soda

1 1/2 tsp. cinnamon
1/4 tsp. nutmeg
1/4 cup wheat germ *or* oat bran, uncooked
1/2 cup raisins
2 cups chopped, unpeeled apple
1/3 cup rolled oats

Beat together oil, honey, egg whites and vanilla. In another bowl, stir together flour, soda, spices and wheat germ (or oat bran). Mix in raisins, apple and oatmeal. Stir flour mixture into honey mixture until well blended.

Coat muffin cups with cooking spray and fill 3/4 full. Bake at 350° for 20 to 25 minutes.

Variation: Spoon batter into an 8" x 8" baking pan coated with cooking spray. Bake at 350° for 40 to 45 minutes.

Yield: 12 to 15 muffins

Per serving:	Calories	Fat (g)	Cholesterol (mg)	Fiber (g)	Sodium (mg)
	133	4	0	2	64

Orange Oatmeal Muffins

Topping:
2 Tbsp. brown sugar
2 tsp. whole wheat flour
1 tsp. liquid margarine
1/4 tsp. cinnamon

Muffins:
1 cup whole wheat flour
1 cup rolled oats
1/4 cup chopped pecans
1/4 cup brown sugar
2 tsp. orange zest
2 tsp. baking powder
1/2 cup orange juice
1/4 cup non-fat milk
3 Tbsp. canola *or* safflower oil
2 egg whites

Prepare Topping: combine brown sugar, 2 tsp. flour, margarine and cinnamon; mix until crumbly. Set aside.

Combine 1 cup flour, oats, pecans, sugar, orange zest, and baking powder. Make a well in the center of the mixture. Combine juice, milk, oil and egg whites. Add to dry ingredients; stir just until moistened.

Spoon mixture into muffin cups coated with cooking spray, filing 3/4 full. Sprinkle with Topping and bake at 425° for 15 to 20 minutes.

Yield: 12 muffins

Per serving:	Calories	Fat (g)	Cholesterol (mg)	Fiber (g)	Sodium (mg)
	141	6	0	2	85

Pineapple Ginger Muffins

1 cup whole wheat flour
1 cup unbleached flour
2 tsp. baking powder
1/2 tsp. baking soda
1/2 tsp. ginger
1/4 tsp. nutmeg

1/4 cup canola *or* safflower oil
1/4 cup honey
2 egg whites
1 8-oz. can crushed pineapple (juice pack), undrained

In a medium bowl, combine flours, baking powder, baking soda, ginger and nutmeg. In a smaller bowl, mix together oil, honey and egg whites. Add to dry ingredients along with pineapple and mix until just blended.

Spoon batter into muffin cups coated with cooking spray, filling 2/3 fill. Bake at 400° for about 20 minutes or until done.

Yield: 12 muffins

Per serving:	Calories	Fat (g)	Cholesterol (mg)	Fiber (g)	Sodium (mg)
	151	5	0	1	112

Sunshine Muffins

1 1/2 cups oat bran
1 cup unbleached flour
1/2 cup whole wheat flour
2 tsp. baking soda
2 tsp. cinnamon
3/4 cup brown sugar
2 cups grated carrots

1 unpeeled apple, cored and grated
1/2 cup raisins
1/4 cup chopped walnuts
6 egg whites
1/2 cup canola *or* safflower oil
2 tsp. vanilla

In a medium bowl, combine first six ingredients, mixing well. Stir in carrots, apple, nuts and raisins. Beat together egg whites, oil and vanilla; then blend into dry ingredients until just mixed.

Coat muffin cups with cooking spray and fill 3/4 full. Bake at 350° for 30 to 35 minutes.

Yield: about 18 muffins.

Per serving:	Calories	Fat (g)	Cholesterol (mg)	Fiber (g)	Sodium (mg)
	191	8	0	3	120

Applesauce Bread

1¹/₂ cups whole wheat flour
¹/₂ cup oat bran
1 tsp. baking soda
1 tsp. cinnamon
¹/₄ tsp. *each* nutmeg and cloves

¹/₂ cup canola *or* safflower oil
¹/₂ cup brown sugar
4 egg whites
2 tsp. vanilla
³/₄ cup unsweetened applesauce

In a large bowl combine flour, oat bran, leavening and spices. In a separate bowl beat together oil, sugar, egg whites and vanilla until fluffy. Add applesauce and blend well.

Add dry ingredients to fruit mixture and stir until combined. Pour batter into 9" x 5" loaf pan coated with cooking spray. Bake at 350° for 65 to 70 minutes or until tester inserted into center comes out clean. Cool in pan 10 minutes. Remove from pan and cool on rack.

Yield: One 9" x 5" loaf, 16 slices; 1 serving = 1 slice

Per serving:	Calories	Fat (g)	Cholesterol (mg)	Fiber (g)	Sodium (mg)
	144	7	0	2	67

Banana Bread

1¹/₂ cups whole wheat flour
¹/₂ cup oat bran
1 tsp. baking soda
1 tsp. *each* cinnamon and cardamon
¹/₂ cup canola *or* safflower oil

¹/₂ cup brown sugar
4 egg whites
2 tsp. vanilla
2 mashed bananas

In a large bowl combine flour, oat bran, baking soda and spices. In a separate bowl beat together oil, sugar, egg whites and vanilla until fluffy. Add bananas and blend well.

Add dry ingredients to fruit mixture and stir until combined. Pour batter into 9" x 5" loaf pan coated with cooking spray. Bake at 350° for 65 to 70 minutes or until tester inserted into center comes out clean. Cool in pan 10 minutes. Remove from pan and cool on rack.

Yield: One 9" x 5" loaf, 16 slices; 1 serving = 1 slice

Per serving:	Calories	Fat (g)	Cholesterol (mg)	Fiber (g)	Sodium (mg)
	152	7	0	2	66

Pumpkin Bread

1¹/₂ cups whole wheat flour
¹/₂ cup oat bran
¹/₂ tsp. *each* baking powder and
   baking soda
¹/₂ tsp. *each* cloves and cinnamon
¹/₄ tsp. nutmeg

¹/₂ cup canola *or* safflower oil
¹/₂ cup brown sugar
4 egg whites
2 tsp. vanilla
1 cup pumpkin

In a large bowl combine flour, oat bran, baking powder, baking soda and spices. In a separate bowl beat together oil, sugar, egg whites and vanilla until fluffy. Add pumpkin and blend well.

Add dry ingredients to fruit mixture and stir until combined. Pour batter into 9" x 5" loaf pan coated with cooking spray. Bake at 350° for 65 to 70 minutes or until tester inserted into center comes out clean. Cool in pan 10 minutes. Remove from pan and cool on rack.

Yield: One 9" x 5" loaf, 16 slices; 1 serving = 1 slice

Per serving:	Calories	Fat (g)	Cholesterol (mg)	Fiber (g)	Sodium (mg)
	145	7	0	2	54

Zucchini Bread

1¹/₂ cups whole wheat flour
¹/₂ cup oat bran
¹/₂ tsp. *each* baking powder and
   baking soda
1 tsp. cinnamon
¹/₄ tsp. cloves

¹/₂ cup canola *or* safflower oil
¹/₂ cup brown sugar
4 egg whites
2 tsp. vanilla
1 cup grated, unpeeled zucchini

In a large bowl combine flour, oat bran, baking powder, baking soda and spices. In a separate bowl beat together oil, sugar, egg whites and vanilla until fluffy. Add zucchini and blend well.

Add dry ingredients to fruit mixture and stir until combined. Pour batter into 9" x 5" loaf pan coated with cooking spray. Bake at 350° for 65 to 70 minutes or until tester inserted into center comes out clean. Cool in pan 10 minutes. Remove from pan and cool on rack.

Yield: One 9" x 5" loaf, 16 slices; 1 serving = 1 slice

Per serving:	Calories	Fat (g)	Cholesterol (mg)	Fiber (g)	Sodium (mg)
	142	7	0	2	54

Cornbread

1/2 cup *each* unbleached and whole
  wheat flour
1 cup cornmeal
2 1/2 tsp. baking powder
1/2 tsp. Lite Salt™ (may be omitted)
4 egg whites

1/4 cup canola *or* safflower oil
2 Tbsp. sugar
1 1/4 cups non-fat milk *or*
  1 cup plain non-fat yogurt and
  1/4 to 1/2 cup non-fat milk

In a medium bowl, blend together flours, cornmeal, baking powder and salt. In a separate bowl beat together egg whites, oil, sugar and milk. Mix into flour mixture until just blended.

Pour batter into an 8" x 8" baking pan coated with cooking spray. Bake at 425° for 20 to 25 minutes. Serve warm.

Serves 12

Variation: Jalapeño Cornbread — omit salt. Add 1 cup whole kernel corn (if canned, salt-free) and 2 to 4 Tbsp. chopped jalapeño or green chile peppers to liquid mixture.

Per serving:	Calories	Fat (g)	Cholesterol (mg)	Fiber (g)	Sodium (mg)
	139	5	1	1	203

Hearty Fruit and Nut Bread

1 1/2-cups unbleached flour
1 1/4 cups whole wheat flour
1/4 cup wheat germ
2 1/2 tsp. baking powder
1 1/2 tsp. cinnamon
1/4 tsp. nutmeg
1 1/3 cups non-fat milk
1/2 cup honey *or* brown sugar

1/4 cup canola *or* safflower oil
2 egg whites
1 cup raisins *or*
  1/2 cup *each* raisins and chopped walnuts
1/4 cup chopped dates
1/4 cup chopped nuts (eliminate if 1/2
  cup walnuts used)

Mix together first 6 ingredients. Beat milk, honey (or brown sugar), oil and egg whites together until light and frothy. Stir fruit and nuts into flour mixture. Add milk mixture and stir just until blended. Pour into a 9" x 5" loaf pan coated with cooking spray. Bake at 325° about one hour or until golden brown.

Yield: One 9" x 5" loaf, 16 slices; 1 serving = 1 slice

Per serving:	Calories	Fat (g)	Cholesterol (mg)	Fiber (g)	Sodium (mg)
	195	5	0	2	84

Peanut Butter Bread

1 cup *each* unbleached and
  whole wheat flour
1 cup rolled oats
3 tsp. baking powder
1 1/2 cups non-fat milk

1/2 cup natural-style peanut butter
1/4 cup honey
3 Tbsp. canola *or* safflower oil
4 egg whites
1/2 cup raisins

Mix flours, oats and baking powder. Blend milk into peanut butter; mix in honey, oil and egg whites. Add to flour mixture; stir until just moistened. Mix in raisins.

Pour batter into a 9" x 5" loaf pan coated with cooking spray. Bake at 375° for 40 to 45 minutes.

Yield: One 9" x 5" loaf, 16 slices; 1 serving = 1 slice

Per serving:	Calories	Fat (g)	Cholesterol (mg)	Fiber (g)	Sodium (mg)
	179	7	0	2	150

Apricot Pineapple Jam

(from "Sugarfree Holidays")

1 15-oz. can pineapple chunks
  (juice pack)
1 6-oz. pkg. dried apricots

1 cup frozen apple juice concentrate, thawed
1/4 tsp. *each* allspice and nutmeg

Drain pineapple juice into medium saucepan. Add apricots, 1/3 cup apple juice concentrate and spices. Simmer, uncovered, 10 minutes. Partially cover, stir occasionally, and simmer until most of the liquid is absorbed and remaining liquid is thickened, about 10 minutes.

Add remaining apple juice concentrate. Bring to a boil then remove from heat. Stir in pineapple chunks. Cool to room temperature then puree. Store, uncovered, in refrigerator.

Delicious on toast, muffins, french toast, pancakes or as a topping for plain yogurt.

Yield: about 2 1/2 cups; 1 serving = 2 Tbsp.

Per serving:	Calories	Fat (g)	Cholesterol (mg)	Fiber (g)	Sodium (mg)
	28	0	0	1	71

Holiday Stuffing

This flavorful dressing is moistened by fresh vegetables rather than butter

1 Tbsp. liquid margarine
1 onion, chopped
4 stalks celery (including tops), chopped
4 to 6 green onions, thinly sliced
1/2 lb. mushrooms, chopped
6 cups bread crumbs (from day old bread)
2 tsp. dried sage

1 tsp. dried marjoram
1/2 tsp. celery salt
1/2 tsp. dried oregano
1/4 tsp. dried thyme
1/2 cup chopped fresh parsley
1/2 cup bourbon (optional)

In a large non-stick skillet, heat margarine. Add chopped vegetables. Cover and cook 5 to 10 minutes or until onions are soft and mushrooms have released some juice. Remove from heat and mix in remaining ingredients. Use to stuff turkey or place in a casserole dish coated with cooking spray and bake at 325° for 30 to 45 minutes. Moisten with salt-free chicken broth as needed during cooking.

Serves 8 to 10

Per serving:	Calories	Fat (g)	Cholesterol (mg)	Fiber (g)	Sodium (mg)
	250	4	0	2	496

Cooking for a Healthier Ever After

Egg Substitute

2 egg whites
1 Tbsp. non-fat dry milk

1 tsp. canola *or* safflower oil
Pinch tumeric (for color, if desired)

Combine ingredients in a blender and blend until smooth. May be used for scrambled eggs and omelettes.

Yield: equivalent of 1 egg

Per serving:	Calories	Fat (g)	Cholesterol (mg)	Fiber (g)	Sodium (mg)
	79	5	0	0	113

Green Chile Omelette

Egg Substitute (above) equal
  to 2 eggs
1 Tbsp. (more or less, to taste) chopped
  green chile
1 corn tortilla

2 to 3 Tbsp. vegetarian refried
  beans *or* black beans
1 to 2 Tbsp. grated low-fat Monterey
  Jack cheese (optional)
Mexican Salsa (page 5)

Beat together egg substitute and green chiles. Pour into a non-stick skillet and cook over low heat until omelette is half-way done. Top with tortilla, beans and cheese. Cover pan and cook 1 to 2 minutes more or until omelette is firm and beans are heated through.

Fold over and slide onto a plate. Top with Salsa.

Serves 1

Per serving:	Calories	Fat (g)	Cholesterol (mg)	Fiber (g)	Sodium (mg)
	242	9	0	3	273

Banana Oatmeal Pancakes

3/4 cup rolled oats
2/3 cup whole wheat flour
1 tsp. baking powder
1/2 tsp. baking soda

1 ripe banana
2 egg whites
3/4 cup low-fat buttermilk
2 Tbsp. canola *or* safflower oil

In a bowl, combine oats, flour, baking powder and baking soda. In another bowl, mash the banana; beat egg whites with banana until blended. Add buttermilk and oil; mix until smooth. Stir in dry ingredients until blended. Cook on a griddle coated with cooking spray.

Yield: 10 pancakes

Per serving:	Calories	Fat (g)	Cholesterol (mg)	Fiber (g)	Sodium (mg)
	186	7	1	3	232

Oatmeal Pancakes

2 egg whites
1 1/4 cups low-fat buttermilk
1 Tbsp. brown sugar *or* honey
2 Tbsp. canola *or* safflower oil

1/2 cup rolled oats
2/3 cup whole wheat flour
2 Tbsp. wheat germ
1/2 tsp. baking soda

Beat together egg whites, buttermilk, brown sugar and oil. Add dry ingredients. If necessary, thin slightly with 1 to 2 Tbsp. non-fat milk.

Pour 1/4 cup of batter onto a griddle coated with cooking spray. Cook over moderate heat until tops begin to bubble and edges are dry. Turn and cook until golden brown.

Yield: Ten to twelve 4" pancakes

Per serving:	Calories	Fat (g)	Cholesterol (mg)	Fiber (g)	Sodium (mg)
	146	5	1	2	153

Orange Pancakes with Orange Sauce

Pancakes:
1 1/2 cups whole wheat flour
2 tsp. baking powder
2 tsp. orange zest
1 egg white
3 Tbsp. honey
1/4 cup non-fat milk
3/4 cup orange juice
1 Tbsp. canola *or* safflower oil

Orange Sauce:
1 Tbsp. cornstarch
2 Tbsp. orange zest
1 cup orange juice
2 to 3 Tbsp. honey
1 orange, peeled and sectioned

Pancakes: Combine flour, baking powder and orange zest. In a separate bowl, combine egg white, honey, milk, orange juice and oil. Stir the wet ingredients into the dry ingredients. Thin batter if needed with orange juice. Bake on a griddle coated with cooking spray.

Yield: 8 to 10 4" pancakes

Per serving:	Calories	Fat (g)	Cholesterol (mg)	Fiber (g)	Sodium (mg)
	101	3	0	0	179

Orange Sauce: Mix cornstarch, orange zest, orange juice and honey in a small sauce pan. Bring to a boil over medium heat, stirring constantly until thickened. Add orange sections. Serve warm.

Yield: 1 cup; 1 serving = 1/4 cup

Per serving:	Calories	Fat (g)	Cholesterol (mg)	Fiber (g)	Sodium (mg)
	90	0	0	1	1

Gingerbread Pancakes with Apple Cinnamon Syrup

Pancakes:
1 1/2 cups whole wheat flour
1 tsp. *each* baking powder and
  baking soda
2 tsp. ginger, minced
1 tsp. allspice
1/4 tsp. cloves
1 egg white
1/4 cup molasses
1/2 cup *each* orange juice and non-fat
  milk *or* 1 cup low-fat buttermilk
1 Tbsp. canola *or* safflower oil

Apple-Cinnamon Syrup:
1 cup frozen apple juice concentrate,
  thawed
1 cup water
1 stick cinnamon
6 whole cloves
1 Golden Delicious apple, cored,
  peeled and sliced
1 Tbsp. cornstarch dissolved in
  1 Tbsp. water

Pancakes: Combine flour, baking powder, baking soda and spices. Add egg white, molasses, orange juice, non-fat milk and oil; blend well.

Cook pancakes on a griddle coated with cooking spray. Serve with Apple-Cinnamon Syrup.

Yield: 10 to 12 pancakes

Per serving:	Calories	Fat (g)	Cholesterol (mg)	Fiber (g)	Sodium (mg)
	177	3	0	3	227

Apple-Cinnamon Syrup: Mix apple juice concentrate, water (or apple juice and honey), cinnamon, cloves and apple slices in a medium saucepan. Bring to a boil. Stir in cornstarch mixture and blend well. Simmer over medium heat for 5 to 10 minutes or until sauce is thickened and apples are soft. Stir often.

Yield: approximately 2 cups; 1 serving = 1/4 cup

Per serving:	Calories	Fat (g)	Cholesterol (mg)	Fiber (g)	Sodium (mg)
	60	0	0	1	1

Sunday Morning Pancakes

1 cup whole wheat flour	2 egg whites
1 tsp. brown sugar *or* honey	1 cup low-fat buttermilk *or* plain non-fat yogurt
1/2 tsp. baking soda	1 Tbsp. canola *or* safflower oil

Mix together dry ingredients. Beat together liquid ingredients and add to dry mixture, stirring until blended.

Pour 1/4 cup batter onto a griddle or pan coated with cooking spray. Cook until bubbly on top and edges are dry. Turn and cook 1 to 2 minutes more or until golden brown.

Yield: about twelve 4" pancakes

Per serving:	Calories	Fat (g)	Cholesterol (mg)	Fiber (g)	Sodium (mg)
	110	3	1	2	139

Baked French Toast

A delicious weekend treat that goes together quickly

1/4 cup liquid margarine	5 egg whites
2 Tbsp. honey	1 cup orange juice
1 tsp. cinnamon	9 slices whole wheat bread
1 egg	

Melt margarine and honey together in a 9" x 13" baking pan. Sprinkle with cinnamon.

Beat together egg, egg whites and orange juice. Dip bread in egg mixture and arrange in baking pan. Bake at 375° for 20 minutes or until set.

Yield: 6 servings, 1 1/2 slices each

Per serving:	Calories	Fat (g)	Cholesterol (mg)	Fiber (g)	Sodium (mg)
	235	10	37	3	348

Peanut Butter French Toast

1/4 cup natural-style peanut butter
3/4 cup non-fat milk

4 egg whites
8 slices whole wheat bread

Place peanut butter, milk and egg whites in a blender or food processor. Blend until smooth. Pour into a shallow dish.

Dip bread into mixture, coating thoroughly. Coat a non-stick griddle with cooking spray. Cook french toast until golden brown on both sides.

Serves 4

Per serving:	Calories	Fat (g)	Cholesterol (mg)	Fiber (g)	Sodium (mg)
	257	10	3	5	428

Waffles

3 egg whites
2 cups low-fat buttermilk
1 cup unbleached flour
1 cup whole wheat flour
1/4 cup wheat germ

2 tsp. baking powder
1 tsp. baking soda
1 tsp. vanilla
1/3 cup canola *or* safflower oil

Heat waffle iron. Lightly beat egg whites until frothy; fold in remaining ingredients until smooth.

Pour batter into center of hot waffle iron. Bake about 5 minutes or until waffle stops steaming. Do not overbake or waffles will be dry.

Yield: Eight 7" waffles

Per serving:	Calories	Fat (g)	Cholesterol (mg)	Fiber (g)	Sodium (mg)
	225	10	1	2	303

Basic Fruit Sauce

Use on pancakes, french toast, waffles or as a topping for yogurt or angel food cake.

2 cups apple juice
2 Tbsp. cornstarch
1 tsp. vanilla

Blend apple juice gradually with cornstarch; cook over medium heat, stirring frequently, until thickened, 4 to 5 minutes. Add vanilla and fruit:

Apple Sauce: add 2 apples, peeled and chopped, and 1 tsp. cinnamon; simmer until apples are soft.

Per serving:	Calories	Fat (g)	Cholesterol (mg)	Fiber (g)	Sodium (mg)
	62	0	0	1	1

Blueberry Sauce: add 1 cup blueberries

Per serving:	Calories	Fat (g)	Cholesterol (mg)	Fiber (g)	Sodium (mg)
	52	0	0	1	1

Orange Sauce: add one cup orange segments and 1 tsp. orange zest

Per serving:	Calories	Fat (g)	Cholesterol (mg)	Fiber (g)	Sodium (mg)
	51	0	0	0	1

Strawberry Sauce: add 1 cup sliced strawberries

Per serving:	Calories	Fat (g)	Cholesterol (mg)	Fiber (g)	Sodium (mg)
	47	0	0	1	1

Yield: 2 cups; 1 serving = 1/4 cup

Cranberry Maple Syrup

2 cups apple juice
2 Tbsp. cornstarch
1 cup cranberries
1 stick cinnamon

6 whole cloves *or*
  1/4 tsp. ground cloves
1/4 cup maple syrup *or*
  1/2 tsp. maple extract

Dissolve cornstarch in 2 to 3 Tbsp. of juice. Combine with remaining juice in a saucepan. Add cranberries, cinnamon stick and cloves. Bring to a boil over high heat, stirring constantly.

Cover and cook over medium heat for 15 to 20 minutes or until cranberries have popped open. Remove cinnamon stick and whole cloves. Add maple syrup or extract.

Yield: 2 cups; 1 serving = 1/4 cup

Per serving:	Calories	Fat (g)	Cholesterol (mg)	Fiber (g)	Sodium (mg)
	140	0	0	1	3

Granola

4 cups rolled oats
1/2 cup *each* wheat germ
  and bran
1/2 cup chopped unsalted, dry-roasted
  nuts *or* 1/2 cup unsalted
  dry-roasted sunflower seeds *or*
  a combination of both

1 1/2 tsp. cinnamon
1/4 cup honey
1/4 cup canola *or* safflower oil
2/3 cup raisins *or* other
  dried fruit

Combine oats, wheat germ, bran, nuts and cinnamon. Heat honey and oil together stirring until well blended (or heat in microwave about one minute stirring until blended). Pour over oat mixture and mix well.

Spread onto baking pan. Bake at 350° for 25 to 30 minutes or until slightly browned, stirring occasionally. Remove from oven and stir in raisins.

To prepare in microwave:

Cook on HIGH for 8 to 10 minutes, stirring every 2 minutes.

Cool, then stir in raisins. Store in air-tight container.

Yield: about 6 cups; 1 serving = 1/2 cup

Per serving:	Calories	Fat (g)	Cholesterol (mg)	Fiber (g)	Sodium (mg)
	259	11	0	10	5

Bircher Muesli

(from the Swiss Bells Restaurant)

2 cups rolled oats
1 cup water
1 whole lemon, seeded and pureed in
  blender or food processor
1/4 cup finely chopped almonds
1/4 cup chopped walnuts
2 cups plain non-fat yogurt

2 cups assorted fresh fruit:
  1 orange, peeled and diced
  1 banana, peeled and diced
  Blueberries
  Kiwi fruit
  Strawberries (add just before serving)
  1 unpeeled apple, diced
  Chopped peaches *or* nectarines
  Raisins
1 to 2 Tbsp. honey *or* brown sugar (optional)

In a large bowl soak rolled oats in cold water for 10 minutes. Add remaining ingredients and mix well. Sweeten, if necessary, with a little honey or brown sugar.

Yield: about 6 cups; 1 serving = 1/2 cup

Per serving:	Calories	Fat (g)	Cholesterol (mg)	Fiber (g)	Sodium (mg)
	140	4	2	3	33

Oatmeal Royale

1 cup orange juice *or* apple juice
11/2 cups water
1/3 cup oat bran
2/3 cup rolled oats

1/4 cup raisins
1/2 tsp. cinnamon
1 unpeeled apple, chopped
1 banana, sliced

Bring water and juice to a boil. Slowly stir in oat bran (to avoid lumping). Add oatmeal, raisins, cinnamon and apple. Cook 5 minutes, stirring occasionally. Add banana and serve.

Per serving:	Calories	Fat (g)	Cholesterol (mg)	Fiber (g)	Sodium (mg)
	168	2	0	5	4

Spiced Oatmeal

2 3/4 cups water
1 tsp. cinnamon
1/4 tsp. *each* nutmeg and allspice

1/3 cup raisins
1/2 cup chopped pitted dates
1 1/3 cups rolled oats

Combine water with spices, raisins and dates. Bring to a boil; stir in oatmeal. Cover and simmer until water is absorbed, 8 to 10 minutes.

Serves 4

Per serving:	Calories	Fat (g)	Cholesterol (mg)	Fiber (g)	Sodium (mg)
	180	2	0	5	4

Apple Rice Cereal

4 cups cooked brown rice
2 cups plain non-fat yogurt
1 Tbsp. brown sugar *or* honey

2 unpeeled apples, cored and chopped
1/2 cup raisins
2 tsp. cinnamon

Combine all ingredients in a saucepan. Simmer until apples are soft.

Serves 6 to 8

Per serving:	Calories	Fat (g)	Cholesterol (mg)	Fiber (g)	Sodium (mg)
	193	2	4	3	319

Baked Apples

4 small apples, cored
¹/₂ cup apple juice
2 Tbsp. raisins

Cinnamon and nutmeg
¹/₂ cup water

Place apples in a baking dish. Fill each cavity with 1 Tbsp. apple juice, and ¹/₂ Tbsp. raisins. Sprinkle with cinnamon and nutmeg.

Pour remaining apple juice and water into baking dish. Bake at 350° or until soft.

Serves 4

Per serving:	Calories	Fat (g)	Cholesterol (mg)	Fiber (g)	Sodium (mg)
	107	1	0	3	2

Fruit Icee

2 cups unsweetened juice
¹/₂ cup non-fat dry milk

¹/₄ tsp. vanilla
8 ice cubes

Combine all ingredients in blender or food processor. Blend until frothy. Serve immediately.

Serves 1

Per serving:	Calories	Fat (g)	Cholesterol (mg)	Fiber (g)	Sodium (mg)
	448	1	12	0	327

Fruit Smoothie

¹/₂ cup frozen fruit
1 cup non-fat yogurt (plain or
** fruit-flavored)**

¹/₂ tsp. cinnamon *or* nutmeg
¹/₄ tsp. vanilla *or* other extract

Place all ingredients in blender or food processor. Blend until smooth.

Serves 1

Per serving:	Calories	Fat (g)	Cholesterol (mg)	Fiber (g)	Sodium (mg)
	177	4	14	0	161

Tropical Banana Shake

$^1/_2$ cup non-fat milk
$^1/_2$ cup plain non-fat yogurt
1 small ripe banana, peeled

$^1/_2$ tsp. vanilla
$^1/_4$ tsp. coconut extract
1 ice cube *or* 2 to 3 frozen strawberries

Combine all ingredients in blender or food processor and blend until smooth.

Serves 1

Per serving:	Calories	Fat (g)	Cholesterol (mg)	Fiber (g)	Sodium (mg)
	398	2	19	2	403

Peanut Butter Banana Shake

1 ripe banana
1$^1/_2$ cups non-fat milk
$^1/_2$ cup rolled oats
2 Tbsp. natural-style peanut butter

1 tsp. honey *or* brown sugar (optional)
1 tsp. vanilla
2 to 3 ice cubes

Cut banana into chunks. Combine with remaining ingredients in blender or food processor container. Cover and blend 1 to 2 minutes or until frothy.

Serves 2

Per serving:	Calories	Fat (g)	Cholesterol (mg)	Fiber (g)	Sodium (mg)
	293	9	4	4	190

Raspberry Frost

1$^1/_2$ cups orange juice
$^1/_2$ cup raspberries, fresh *or* frozen
   (unsweetened)

1 egg white
1 cup crushed ice

Combine all ingredients except ice in a blender or food processor. Blend about 30 seconds. Gradually add ice, blending until thick and frothy.

Serves 4

Per serving:	Calories	Fat (g)	Cholesterol (mg)	Fiber (g)	Sodium (mg)
	225	1	0	3	55

Orange Julie

(an Orange Julius-type drink)

1 12-oz. can frozen orange
  juice concentrate, thawed
2 cups non-fat milk
2 cups pineapple juice

4 cups crushed ice
2$^1/_2$ cups water
2 tsp. vanilla

Combine ingredients in blender and mix until smooth. (Refrigerate what isn't consumed right away, and then shake and RE-BLEND each serving just before drinking — it's better when it has just been "revved" in the blender and is foamy!)

Yield: 10 to 12 cups; 1 serving = 1 cup

Per serving:	Calories	Fat (g)	Cholesterol (mg)	Fiber (g)	Sodium (mg)
	83	0	1	0	22

Spiced Cocoa Mix

1$^1/_2$ cups non-fat dry milk
$^1/_3$ cup sugar
$^1/_3$ cup cocoa powder
$^1/_4$ cup instant decaffeinated coffee
  (optional)

$^1/_2$ tsp. cinnamon
$^1/_4$ tsp. *each* nutmeg and cloves

Combine all ingredients. Store in airtight jar. To serve, place 1 heaping tablespoon in a cup. Add boiling water to fill (about 6 oz.). Stir until completely blended.

Yield: about 40 servings; 1 serving = 1 Tbsp.

Per serving:	Calories	Fat (g)	Cholesterol (mg)	Fiber (g)	Sodium (mg)
	23	0	1	0	25

Cooking for a Healthier Ever After

Marinara Sauce

1 onion, chopped
2 cloves garlic, minced
1 Tbsp. olive oil
1/2 lb. mushrooms, sliced
1 *or* 2 carrots, grated
1 *or* 2 zucchini, grated

1 green *or* red bell pepper, chopped
2 28-oz. cans salt-free tomatoes, chopped
1/4 cup dry red wine (optional)
1 tsp. *each* basil and oregano
1/4 tsp. thyme
1/4 cup chopped fresh parsley

Saute onion and garlic in olive oil until soft. Add mushrooms, carrot, zucchini and green pepper; cook 3 to 4 minutes, stirring.

Add remaining ingredients and simmer, covered, for 45 to 60 minutes; stir occasionally. Serve over eggless pasta or use in Lasagne (page 62).

Yield: about 6 cups; 1 serving = 1 cup

Per serving:	Calories	Fat (g)	Cholesterol (mg)	Fiber (g)	Sodium (mg)
	124	3	0	8	65

Eggplant Sauce

1 unpeeled eggplant (about 1 pound),
   diced
1 cup sliced mushrooms
2 cloves garlic, minced
3 shallots *or* 1/4 cup minced onion
1/4 tsp. crushed red pepper flakes

1 to 2 Tbsp. olive oil
2 cups canned salt-free tomatoes,
   undrained and chopped *or*
   2 fresh tomatoes, cored and chopped
1/4 cup chopped fresh parsley *or* 1 Tbsp. dried

Saute eggplant, mushrooms, garlic, shallots and red bell pepper in oil for 8 to 10 minutes, stirring often. Add tomatoes and parsley. Simmer, covered, for 15 to 20 minutes. Serve over eggless pasta.

Serves 6

Per serving:	Calories	Fat (g)	Cholesterol (mg)	Fiber (g)	Sodium (mg)
	78	4	0		21

Red Pepper Coulis

Coulis is another name for a thick puree. Serve this sauce over pasta, fish, chicken or steamed vegetables.

5 red bell peppers, seeded and
  coarsely chopped
1/2 cup salt-free chicken broth, defatted

2 Tbsp. Balsamic vinegar
2 cloves garlic, minced
2 tsp. basil

In a food processor or blender, puree the peppers, broth, vinegar, garlic and basil until smooth. Pour into a medium saucepan and bring to a boil. Lower the heat slightly and cook uncovered for 10 minutes, until sauce is thick and fragrant.

Yield: 2 cups; one serving = 1/2 cup.

Per serving:	Calories	Fat (g)	Cholesterol (mg)	Fiber (g)	Sodium (mg)
	25	0	0	1	14

Spaghetti Bolognese

2 lbs. ground turkey *or* lean ground beef
2 cups finely chopped onions
2 cups sliced mushrooms
4 cloves garlic, minced
1 Tbsp. olive oil
2 28-oz. cans Italian tomatoes, chopped
2 6-oz. cans salt-free tomato paste

1 cup dry red wine *or*
  1 cup salt-free beef broth
1 Tbsp. *each* oregano and basil
1 tsp. thyme
1 bay leaf
1/2 cup chopped fresh parsley
1 tsp. black pepper

Brown ground turkey, onion, mushrooms and garlic in olive oil. Add remaining ingredients. Bring to a boil; reduce heat and simmer 1 to 1 1/2 hours, stirring occasionally. Serve over egg-less pasta.

Serves 12

Per serving:	Calories	Fat (g)	Cholesterol (mg)	Fiber (g)	Sodium (mg)
	190	4	17	4	274

Joe's Spaghetti With Clam Sauce

2 cloves garlic, minced
2 Tbsp. olive oil
1 7-oz. can clams with liquid
1/2 tsp. *each* oregano and basil

Optional: 2 cups broccoli florets,
  steamed until tender-crisp
8 oz. eggless spaghetti
Parmesan cheese, grated

Saute garlic in olive oil until golden. Add clams with liquid, oregano and broccoli.

Cook spaghetti according to package directions, omitting salt; drain. Pour sauce over cooked spaghetti and toss to mix. Sprinkle lightly with Parmesan cheese.

Serves 3 to 4

Per serving:	Calories	Fat (g)	Cholesterol (mg)	Fiber (g)	Sodium (mg)
	305	4	40	0	119

Red Clam Sauce

1/2 cup *each* chopped celery and onion
2 cloves garlic, minced
1 Tbsp. olive oil
1 10-oz. can clams
1 16-oz. can salt-free whole tomatoes,
  chopped

1 6-oz. can salt-free tomato paste
1 bay leaf
1 tsp. *each* basil and oregano
1/4 tsp. thyme
2 Tbsp. chopped fresh parsley *or* 2 tsp. dried

Saute onion, celery and garlic in olive oil until soft. Drain clams, reserving liquid.

Add clam liquid, tomatoes, tomato paste, bay leaf and herbs to pan. Bring to a boil. Reduce heat and simmer, partially covered, for 45 minutes. Stir in clams and continue cooking 1 to 2 minutes just to heat clams. (Do not overcook or clams will be tough.) Remove bay leaf.

Serve over eggless pasta.

Serves 6 to 8

Per serving:	Calories	Fat (g)	Cholesterol (mg)	Fiber (g)	Sodium (mg)
	106	3	24	2	73

Pasta With Salmon

1 Tbsp. olive oil
1 onion, chopped
1 red *or* green pepper, chopped
1 tsp. thyme
1/2 tsp. oregano

1 7 1/2-oz. can salmon, drained and flaked
8 oz. eggless pasta, cooked and drained
1 10-oz. pkg. frozen peas, thawed
1/3 cup Parmesan cheese

Heat olive oil in a large skillet. Saute onion, pepper, thyme and oregano until soft, then stir in salmon and cook until heated through. Toss with pasta and peas.

Sprinkle with Parmesan cheese and serve.

Serves 4 to 6

Per serving:	Calories	Fat (g)	Cholesterol (mg)	Fiber (g)	Sodium (mg)
	275	7	29	2	243

Fettucini "Alfredo"

4 oz. eggless fettucini
1 cup 1% cottage cheese
2 Tbsp. Parmesan cheese
1 Tbsp. cornstarch

2 tsp. butter flavored sprinkles (e.g. Butter Buds)
1/4 tsp. garlic powder
Black pepper

Cook fettucini according to package directions, omitting salt. While pasta is cooking, prepare sauce: combine remaining ingredients in food processor (or blender) and process until **very** smooth, 3 to 4 minutes.

Drain fettucini and cool slightly. Mix with sauce and serve immediately (sauce separates if it stands too long). Add pepper to taste.

Serves 2

Per serving:	Calories	Fat (g)	Cholesterol (mg)	Fiber (g)	Sodium (mg)
	327	4	11	0	515

Fettucini With Seafood Sauce

2 cloves garlic, minced
2 Tbsp. soft margarine
4 Tbsp. unbleached flour
1/2 tsp. Lite Salt™
1/4 tsp. black pepper
2 cups non-fat milk

1 cup salt-free chicken broth, defatted
2 Tbsp. Marsala wine (optional)
8 oz. scallops, cooked
4 oz. shrimp, cooked
12 oz. fettucini (eggless)
2 Tbsp. Parmesan cheese

Saute garlic in margarine until soft but not browned. Stir in flour, salt and pepper; cook until bubbly. Add milk, chicken broth and wine, stirring constantly; cook until thickened. Add scallops and shrimp. Cook, stirring frequently, 2 minutes more.

Cook fettucini according to package directions, omitting salt; drain. Toss sauce with fettucini. Sprinkle with Parmesan cheese and serve.

Serves 6

Per serving:	Calories	Fat (g)	Cholesterol (mg)	Fiber (g)	Sodium (mg)
	353	5	54	0	436

Lasagne

1/2 lb. ground turkey *or*
  lean ground beef
1 onion, chopped
2 stalks celery (including tops), chopped
2 carrots, chopped
2 cloves garlic, minced
1 28-oz. can crushed tomatoes
1 16-oz. can salt-free whole tomatoes,
  chopped
1 12-oz. can salt-free tomato paste
2 tsp. basil
1 tsp. oregano
1/2 tsp. fennel seeds, crushed
1/2 tsp. Lite Salt™
1/2 tsp. black pepper
1/4 tsp. thyme
8 oz. lasagne noodles (eggless)

Cheese filling:
2 cups low-fat ricotta cheese
2 cups 1% cottage cheese
1/4 lb. part-skim mozzarella cheese,
  grated
2 Tbsp. chopped fresh parsley
2 egg whites
1/3 cup Parmesan cheese

Cook ground turkey, onion, celery, carrots and garlic in a skillet over medium heat until turkey is no longer pink. Add tomatoes, tomato paste, herbs, salt and pepper; simmer 30 minutes or until thickened.

Meanwhile, make cheese filling: in a large bowl combine ricotta, cottage cheese, mozzarella, egg whites and parsley. Mix well and set aside.

Cook noodles al dente according to package directions, omitting salt. Set aside.

To assemble: Coat a 9" x 13" baking dish with cooking spray. Spread half the sauce on the bottom. Cover with half the noodles, then spread with the cheese filling. Cover with remaining noodles and sauce. Cover lightly with foil. Bake at 350° for 25 minutes. Uncover, sprinkle with Parmesan cheese and bake another 10 to 15 minutes or until heated through.

Note: If cottage cheese is watery, drain in a colander before using.

Serves 10 to 12

Per serving:	Calories	Fat (g)	Cholesterol (mg)	Fiber (g)	Sodium (mg)
	246	7	35	3	476

Herbed Rice Pilaf

1 cup minced onion
1 cup raw brown rice
2 tsp. olive oil
2 cups salt-free, defatted chicken broth

1 tsp. parsley
1/4 tsp. thyme
1/4 tsp. Lite Salt™

In a saucepan saute onion and rice in olive oil until onion is soft, about 5 minutes. Add broth, herbs and salt. Bring to a boil. Cover; reduce heat and simmer 50 to 60 minutes or until water is absorbed and rice is tender.

Serves 4 to 6

Per serving:	Calories	Fat (g)	Cholesterol (mg)	Fiber (g)	Sodium (mg)
	141	2	0	2	97

Wild Rice Pilaf

(from the Brown Palace Hotel)

1 tsp. olive oil
1/3 cup chopped onions
1/2 cup sliced mushrooms
1 cup raw wild rice, rinsed

3 1/2 cups salt-free chicken broth, defatted
2 bay leaves
1/4 tsp. black pepper
1/4 cup pine nuts

Heat oil in a large skillet. Saute onions, mushrooms and rice until onion is soft, 3 to 4 minutes. Add broth, bay leaves and pepper. Bring to a boil, reduce heat and simmer, covered, 30 to 45 minutes or until rice is tender (or cover and bake 1 hour).

Brown pine nuts lightly in a small skillet and stir into cooked rice before serving.

Serves 4

Per serving:	Calories	Fat (g)	Cholesterol (mg)	Fiber (g)	Sodium (mg)
	136	6	0	2	33

Barley Casserole

1 lb. mushrooms, chopped
1 onion, chopped *or*
  6 green onions, thinly sliced
1 Tbsp. liquid margarine *or* olive oil

1 cup barley
2 cups salt-free chicken broth, defatted
1/4 tsp. black pepper
2 Tbsp. chopped fresh parsley

Saute mushrooms and onions in margarine for 4 to 5 minutes. Add barley and cook, stirring, for 1 to 2 minutes. Transfer to a 1 1/2 quart baking dish. Add broth, pepper and parsley.

Cover tightly. Bake at 350° for 50 to 60 minutes or until barley is tender and liquid is absorbed. Barley may also be cooked on top of stove, tightly covered, for 45 minutes.

Serves 8

Per serving:	Calories	Fat (g)	Cholesterol (mg)	Fiber (g)	Sodium (mg)
	60	2	0	5	33

Bulgur Pilaf

Bulgur is cracked wheat that has been pre-cooked, then dried. It cooks quickly and is a delicious change from rice.

1/2 cup bulgur, uncooked
1 Tbsp. sesame seeds
1 cup salt-free, defatted beef *or*
  chicken broth

2 Tbsp. minced parsley
1/2 tsp. Lite Salt™

Place bulgur and sesame seeds in a medium saucepan. Toast over medium heat, stirring often until sesame seeds are golden. Add broth, parsley and salt. Bring to a boil, then reduce heat and simmer, covered, for 15 to 20 minutes or until liquid is absorbed.

Variation: Substitute couscous for bulgur; reduce cooking time to 5 to 10 minutes.

Serves 2 to 3

Per serving:	Calories	Fat (g)	Cholesterol (mg)	Fiber (g)	Sodium (mg)
	129	2	0	0	3

Mexicali Rice

1 Tbsp. olive oil
1/2 cup onion
1/2 cup diced green *or* red bell pepper
1 clove garlic
1 cup raw brown rice
3 cups salt-free chicken *or* beef broth, defatted

1/2 cup salt-free tomato paste
1/2 tsp. oregano
1/4 tsp. thyme
1/4 tsp. black pepper
Pinch cumin

Heat oil in a medium saucepan. Saute onion, green pepper, garlic and rice until onion is soft, about 5 minutes. Add broth, tomato paste, oregano, thyme, pepper and cumin; bring to a boil. Cover, reduce heat and cook over low heat for 40 to 45 minutes or until all liquid is absorbed.

Serves 4 to 6

Per serving:	Calories	Fat (g)	Cholesterol (mg)	Fiber (g)	Sodium (mg)
	155	3	0	2	17

Tabouli

1 cup bulgur, uncooked
2 cups hot water
3 tomatoes, cored and chopped
1 cucumber, seeded and chopped
6 green onions, thinly sliced
1/2 cup chopped fresh parsley
2 Tbsp. fresh mint, minced *or*
 2 tsp. dried mint

1/4 cup lemon juice
2 Tbsp. olive oil
1/2 tsp. oregano
1/2 tsp. black pepper
1/4 tsp. celery salt

Combine bulgur and water in a bowl and soak 1 hour. Drain well.

Add remaining ingredients to bulgur, mixing well. Serve at room temperature or chilled. May be served in a tomato half or in pita bread.

Variations:

•1/4 cup sunflower seeds (dry roasted, unsalted)

•1 cup garbanzo or kidney beans

•1 61/2-oz. can water packed tuna

•Plain, non-fat yogurt

•1/2 cup grated carrots and/or jicama

Serves 4 to 6

Per serving:	Calories	Fat (g)	Cholesterol (mg)	Fiber (g)	Sodium (mg)
	171	5	0	1	69

Entrees

Salads

The delectable bean — a great source of complex carbohydrate, fiber, protein, iron and vitamins. All this nutrition for about 100 calories per one-half cup; one ounce of steak — which is just a bite or two — contains the same number of calories with saturated fat and cholesterol as well.

Unfortunately the humble bean is often neglected because of the long cooking time required. But with some planning beans can assume a place of honor on your dinner table.

Proper soaking not only reduces cooking time but eliminates much of the gas many people suffer when eating beans. Cooking beans in fresh water is the key.

Cleaning: Rinse dry beans or peas in cold water; discard small stones and discolored or shriveled beans.

Soaking: (Quick method) In a large pan cover each cup of beans with 3 cups water. Bring to a boil and boil for 2 minutes. Cover and let soak 1 hour. Discard water, and add fresh, 3 to 4 cups per cup of beans. Proceed with recipe.

(Overnight soaking) In a large pan combine beans and water in the same proportion as above. Soak overnight. Discard water and replace with fresh water. Proceed with recipe.

Confetti Bean Salad

1/4 lb. fresh green beans
1 16-oz. can salt-free kidney beans,
   drained
1 16-oz. can garbanzo beans,
   rinsed and drained

1 12-oz. can salt-free corn
1/2 cup chopped red and/or green pepper
1/2 cup chopped red onion
1 clove garlic, minced
1/3 cup Vinaigrette Dressing (page 29)

Wash beans and slice into 1" pieces. Steam until tender crisp. Cool.

Combine with remaining ingredients, blending well. Chill before serving.

Serves 6 to 8

Per serving:	Calories	Fat (g)	Cholesterol (mg)	Fiber (g)	Sodium (mg)
	207	7	0	8	25

Tuna Bean Salad

2 cups cooked or canned (salt-free) Great
   Northern, garbanzo *or* kidney beans
1 6 1/2-oz. can low-sodium, water-packed
   tuna, drained
1/2 red or green pepper, julienne

1/4 cup minced red onion *or*
   2 green onions, thinly sliced
2 Tbsp. chopped fresh parsley
1 tsp. basil
1/4 cup Vinaigrette Dressing (page 29)

Combine all ingredients in a medium bowl. Toss lightly to combine.

Serve garnished with tomato wedges, cucumber slices and black olives.

Serves 2 to 4

Per serving:	Calories	Fat (g)	Cholesterol (mg)	Fiber (g)	Sodium (mg)
	240	9	29	10	432

Tuscan Salad

2 15-oz. cans Great Northern beans,
  rinsed and drained
1 red onion, chopped *or*
  6 green onions, thinly sliced
1 cup chopped celery, including tops

1/4 cup chopped fresh parsley
2 to 3 tomatoes, cored and chopped
1/2 tsp. *each* sage, basil and oregano
1/4 cup olive oil
3 Tbsp. lemon juice

Combine all ingredients and mix gently. Serve on a lettuce lined platter or serving bowl garnished with tomato wedges and fresh parsley.

Serves 6 to 8

Per serving:	Calories	Fat (g)	Cholesterol (mg)	Fiber (g)	Sodium (mg)
	195	7	0	11	24

Quick Chili Con Carne

1/2 cup chopped onion
1/2 cup chopped green pepper
1/2 lb. lean ground beef *or* ground turkey
1 15-oz. can salt-free tomato sauce
1 15-oz. can salt-free whole *or*
  stewed tomatoes

2 15-oz. cans salt-free kidney beans, drained
1/2 to 1 tsp. chili powder
1/4 tsp. *each* cumin and black pepper
1/4 tsp. dry mustard

Combine onion, green pepper and crumbled ground beef or turkey in a plastic colander placed in a 2 quart glass casserole. Microwave on full power for 6 minutes, stirring every 2 minutes. Pour off drippings. Transfer mixture to casserole dish. Add remaining ingredients. Microwave on full power covered, for 10 to 12 minutes, stirring halfway through cooking. Let stand, covered, for 5 minutes before serving.

Serves 4 to 6

Per serving:	Calories	Fat (g)	Cholesterol (mg)	Fiber (g)	Sodium (mg)
	244	2	25	16	66

Vegetarian Chili

1/2 cup bulgur
1 cup salt-free tomato sauce
1 cup water *or* low-sodium,
  defatted beef broth
1 onion, chopped
2 to 3 cloves garlic, minced
1 Tbsp. olive oil
1 cup *each* chopped celery, carrots
  and green pepper

2 cups chopped fresh tomatoes *or*
  1 32-oz. can salt-free tomatoes, chopped
5 cups cooked pinto beans (if canned,
  salt-free)
1 to 2 Tbsp. chili powder
2 tsp. cumin
1 tsp. oregano
Dash cayenne (to taste)

Combine bulgur with tomato sauce and water (or beef broth). Let stand 15 to 20 minutes to soften.

In a large saucepan, saute onions and garlic in olive oil until soft. Add remaining ingredients, including bulgur, and simmer, covered, until vegetables are tender and chili is of desired thickness, 30 to 60 minutes. Add water as needed. Stir occasionally.

Serve with Cornbread (page 65), warm corn tortillas or whole wheat rolls.

Serves 6 to 8

Per serving:	Calories	Fat (g)	Cholesterol (mg)	Fiber (g)	Sodium (mg)
	337	3	0	17	60

Chili with Vegetables

Delicious served over brown rice

1/2 cup bulgur
1 cup hot water
1 red onion, chopped
1 white onion, chopped
1 Tbsp. olive oil
3 garlic cloves, minced
1/2 cup *each* chopped celery and carrot
1 to 2 Tbsp. chili powder
1 to 2 Tbsp. (or less, if desired) cumin

1/2 tsp. cayenne pepper
2 tsp. *each* basil and oregano
1 *each* yellow squash and zucchini, cubed
1 *each* green and red bell pepper, diced
1 cup mushrooms, sliced
2 15-oz. cans salt-free kidney beans, undrained
1 15-oz. can salt-free tomatoes
3/4 cup white wine *or* salt-free,
   defatted beef broth

Combine bulgur and hot water. Let soak 30 minutes to soften.

Saute onions in oil until soft. Add garlic, celery and carrots; saute 3 to 4 minutes. Add chili powder, cumin, cayenne, basil and oregano. Cook, covered, over low heat until carrots are almost tender.

Add yellow squash, zucchini, green and red bell peppers, mushrooms, beans, tomatoes, wine and bulgur. Simmer, covered, 30 minutes or until vegetables are tender.

Serves 8

Per serving:	Calories	Fat (g)	Cholesterol (mg)	Fiber (g)	Sodium (mg)
	186	3	0	8	58

Black Bean Enchiladas

1 Tbsp. olive oil
1 onion, chopped
1 green *or* red bell pepper,
  seeded and diced.
3 cloves garlic, minced
1 16-oz. can black beans,
  drained and rinsed

1 7-oz. can salt-free corn, drained
1 tsp. oregano
1/2 tsp. cumin
2 cups salsa, divided
8 corn tortillas
1/2 cup grated low-fat Monterey Jack
  cheese

Heat olive oil in a large skillet; saute onion, pepper and garlic until soft, 2 to 3 minutes. Add beans, corn, oregano, cumin and 1/2 cup salsa. Cook 3 to 4 minutes; mash beans slightly.

Heat tortillas to soften for rolling: moisten each lightly and stack between paper towels. Wrap in foil then heat for 10 minutes at 350°. Or place tortillas in a plastic bag and microwave 1 1/2 to 2 minutes.

Spoon 1/2 cup salsa into a 9" x 13" baking dish coated with cooking spray. Spoon 1/3 cup filling onto each tortilla. Roll up and place seam side down in baking dish. Top with remaining salsa. Cover with foil. Bake at 350° for 15 to 20 minutes. Uncover and sprinkle with cheese. Bake 2 to 3 minutes longer or until cheese is melted.

Yield: 8 enchiladas; 1 serving = 1 enchilada

Per serving:	Calories	Fat (g)	Cholesterol (mg)	Fiber (g)	Sodium (mg)
	233	7	8	2	400

Five Bean Casserole

Rinsing canned beans removes much of the salt. Drain well before using.

1 lb. ground turkey
1 onion, chopped
2 cloves garlic, minced
1 Tbsp. mustard
1/2 cup low-sodium catsup
2 Tbsp. cider vinegar
1/2 cup brown sugar
2 16-oz. cans salt-free tomato sauce

1 16-oz. can salt-free corn
1 16 oz. can garbanzo beans, rinsed and drained
1 16-oz. can lima beans, rinsed and drained
1 16-oz. can Great Northern beans, rinsed and drained
1 16-oz. can salt-free kidney beans
1 16-oz. can vegetarian baked beans

In a large pot, cook ground turkey, onion and garlic until turkey loses its pink color and onions are soft. Drain if necessary.

Add remaining ingredients and mix well. Cover and simmer for one hour.

Variation: Substitute (or add) other canned beans.

Serves 14 to 16; 1 serving = 1 cup

Per serving:	Calories	Fat (g)	Cholesterol (mg)	Fiber (g)	Sodium (mg)
	411	4	18	19	291

Colorado Baked Beans

1 lb. dry anasazi beans, washed
2 cups orange juice
2 cups water
1 8-oz. can salt-free tomato sauce

3/4 cup chopped onion
1/4 cup molasses
2 Tbsp. Worcestershire sauce
2 tsp. liquid smoke

Soak beans according to directions on page 98. Discard soaking water.

Mix all ingredients in a three-quart ovenproof dish. Bake, covered, at 300° for three hours or until beans are softened but still firm. Increase heat to 325°. Remove 1/2 cup of beans and mash. Return to pan. Cook, uncovered about 30 minutes longer or until sauce has thickened.

Note: Beans will be firm when done.

Yield: 8 to 10 servings

Per serving:	Calories	Fat (g)	Cholesterol (mg)	Fiber (g)	Sodium (mg)
	111	0	0	5	42

Beans and Rice

1 onion, chopped
2 cloves garlic, minced
1 green *or* red bell pepper, chopped
1 cup chopped celery
1 cup carrots, chopped or grated
2 zucchini, chopped or grated
1 Tbsp. olive oil

1 16-oz. can salt-free kidney beans, undrained
1/4 cup chopped fresh parsley
1 tsp. *each* basil and oregano
1/2 tsp. Lite Salt™
Black pepper to taste
2 tomatoes, cored and diced
5 cups cooked brown rice

Saute onion, garlic, peppers, celery, carrots and zucchini in oil until soft. Add beans, parsley and seasonings. Cover and simmer 30 minutes. Stir in diced tomatoes. Serve over brown rice.

Sprinkle lightly with Parmesan cheese if desired.

Serves 6

Per serving:	Calories	Fat (g)	Cholesterol (mg)	Fiber (g)	Sodium (mg)
	340	4	0	12	587

Apple Bean Bake

2 15-oz. cans vegetarian baked beans
2 Tbsp. molasses
2 Tbsp. cider vinegar

2 Tbsp. Dijon mustard
2 unpeeled cored apples (one chopped, one sliced)

Combine all ingredients except apple slices in a 2 quart casserole; blend well. Arrange apple slices on top.

Cover and bake at 350° for 30 minutes. Uncover and bake 30 minutes longer.

Serves 6 to 8

Per serving:	Calories	Fat (g)	Cholesterol (mg)	Fiber (g)	Sodium (mg)
	124	1	0	3	428

Hearty Bean and Cornbread Casserole

1 15-oz. can salt-free pinto beans,
  drained
1 15-oz. can salt-free kidney beans,
  drained
3/4 cup chopped green pepper
1/2 cup chopped onion

1/4 cup low-sodium chile sauce *or* catsup
1 8-oz. can salt-free tomato sauce
1 tsp. dry mustard *or*
  1 Tbsp. prepared mustard
1 recipe Cornbread (page 65)
1 81/2-oz. can cream-style corn

Combine first 7 ingredients and pour into a 9" x 13" baking dish coated with cooking spray.

Prepare Cornbread, adding cream-style corn. Spread evenly over bean mixture to within 1" of edge. Bake at 375° for 30 to 35 minutes or until cornbread is done.

Serves 8

Per serving:	Calories	Fat (g)	Cholesterol (mg)	Fiber (g)	Sodium (mg)
	408	8	2	14	430

Garbanzo Hot Pot

1 onion, chopped
1 to 2 cloves garlic, minced
1 Tbsp. olive oil
2 15-oz. cans garbanzo beans, undrained

3 Tbsp. vinegar
1 green pepper, chopped
1 6-oz. can salt-free tomato paste
1/2 cup chopped fresh parsley

In a medium saucepan saute onion and garlic in oil until soft. Add remaining ingredients and simmer, cover, for 30 to 45 minutes.

Serves 6 to 8

Per serving:	Calories	Fat (g)	Cholesterol (mg)	Fiber (g)	Sodium (mg)
	181	4	0	3	25

Felafel

A great filling for a pita sandwich; make smaller size for appetizers.

4 cups cooked garbanzo beans
  (if canned, rinse and drain)
3 cloves garlic
1 to 2 stalks celery, including tops,
  chopped
1/2 cup chopped onion

2 egg whites
1 to 2 Tbsp. tahini (sesame seed paste) *or*
  1 Tbsp. olive oil
3 Tbsp. dry bread crumbs
1/2 tsp. *each* cumin and turmeric
1/4 tsp. *each* cayenne and salt

Process beans in blender or food processor until smooth. Add remaining ingredients and process again until well mixed. Chill.

Form mixture into 1" balls (oil your hands if necessary to prevent batter from sticking). Place on non-stick baking sheet coated with cooking spray. Bake at 350° until golden brown, about 15 minutes.

Serve hot in pita bread with sliced cucumber, sliced tomato and alfalfa sprouts. Top with plain, non-fat yogurt.

Yield: about a dozen 1" balls; 1 serving = 1 felafel ball

Per serving:	Calories	Fat (g)	Cholesterol (mg)	Fiber (g)	Sodium (mg)
	224	5	0	3	144

Fish

Sea Bass with Ginger Sauce

1 1/2 lbs. sea bass fillets
1/2 Tbsp. peanut oil
2 Tbsp. minced fresh ginger

1 Tbsp. low-sodium soy sauce
2 Tbsp. chopped cilantro

Place fish on a steamer rack. Cover and steam until fish flakes easily with a fork, about 8 to 10 minutes per inch of thickness.

In a small pan, heat oil. Saute ginger until crisp, 2 to 3 minutes. Place fish on serving plate. Pour on gingered oil; sprinkle with soy sauce and cilantro.

Serves 4

Per serving:	Calories	Fat (g)	Cholesterol (mg)	Fiber (g)	Sodium (mg)
	185	5	70	0	267

Salsa Baked Cod

1 cup salsa
1/4 cup chopped fresh cilantro
2 lbs. cod fillets

Combine salsa and cilantro. Place cod in a baking dish coated with cooking spray. Pour salsa over fish. Bake at 400° until fish flakes easily with a fork, 8 to 10 minutes per inch of thickness.

Serves 4 to 6

Per serving:	Calories	Fat (g)	Cholesterol (mg)	Fiber (g)	Sodium (mg)
	267	9	77	0	357

Orange Ginger Cod

1/2 cup low-sugar orange marmalade
2 green onions, minced
2 tsp. lemon juice

1 tsp. minced fresh ginger
1 tsp. low-sodium soy sauce
2 lbs. cod fillets

Combine all ingredients except fish. Place fish in a shallow casserole dish coated with cooking spray. Spread sauce over fish. Bake at 400° until fish flakes easily with a fork, 8 to 10 minutes per inch of thickness.

Serves 4 to 6

Per serving:	Calories	Fat (g)	Cholesterol (mg)	Fiber (g)	Sodium (mg)
	288	8	77	0	213

Sweet and Sour Cod

1 lb. cod *or* other firm white fish such as halibut, swordfish *or* turbot)
1 tsp. soft margarine
1 tsp. lemon juice
1 tsp. cornstarch
2 Tbsp. *each* unsweetened pineapple juice and vinegar

1 Tbsp. low-sodium soy sauce
1 cup sliced celery
1/2 cup juice-pack pineapple chunks (reserve 2 Tbsp. juice for sauce)

Place fish in a 8" x 8" baking dish coated with cooking spray. Drizzle with margarine and lemon juice. Bake, uncovered, at 450° for 8 to 10 minutes or until fish flakes easily with a fork.

Prepare sauce while fish is cooking. In a saucepan combine cornstarch with pineapple juice, vinegar and soy sauce. Cook and stir over high heat one minute or until thickened. Add celery and pineapple chunks. Cover and cook over medium heat 3 to 5 minutes, stirring occasionally, until celery is tender crisp. Serve over fish.

Serves 4

Per serving:	Calories	Fat (g)	Cholesterol (mg)	Fiber (g)	Sodium (mg)
	238	7	58	0	314

Monterey Bay Fish and Rice

2 cups water
1 cup raw brown rice
1/2 tsp. Lite Salt™
1/2 cup chopped celery, including tops
2 green onions, thinly sliced
1 cup sliced mushrooms
2 cloves garlic, minced

2 tsp. olive oil
1 cup dry white wine
1/4 cup salt-free tomato paste
1 tsp. thyme
1 1/2 lbs. cod, halibut *or* other white fish,
   cut into serving pieces
1 tomato, chopped

Combine water, rice, salt and celery in a saucepan. Bring to a boil. Cover tightly and cook over low heat until water is absorbed, 45 to 50 minutes.

Meanwhile, saute onion, mushrooms and garlic in oil until soft. Add wine, tomato paste and thyme. Simmer, covered, for 30 minutes. Add fish. Cook 10 to 12 minutes longer or until fish flakes easily with fork. Stir in tomato.

Spoon rice onto platter. Arrange fish on top and pour sauce over.

Serves 6

Per serving:	Calories	Fat (g)	Cholesterol (mg)	Fiber (g)	Sodium (mg)
	274	8	15	3	77

Oriental Seafood Stir-Fry

1/3 cup dry white wine
2 Tbsp. low-sodium soy sauce
1 tsp. minced fresh ginger
2 cloves garlic, minced
1 tsp. cornstarch
1/2 tsp. onion powder
1/2 tsp. black pepper
1 Tbsp. Oriental sesame oil

1 lb. halibut, swordfish, orange roughy,
   monkfish, or other white fish,
   cut into 1" pieces
1 to 2 tsp. canola *or* safflower oil
2 cups sliced mushrooms
1 cup celery, sliced on the diagonal
1/2 cup sliced green onion
1 cup broccoli, cut into bite-size pieces

Combine wine, soy sauce, ginger, garlic, cornstarch, onion powder, pepper and sesame oil. Add fish and marinate for 15 minutes.

Heat oil in wok. Stir-fry vegetables until tender-crisp. Add fish and marinade; continue stir-frying until fish is done (flakes easily with a fork). Serve with brown rice.

Serves 4

Per serving:	Calories	Fat (g)	Cholesterol (mg)	Fiber (g)	Sodium (mg)
	243	14	23	3	416

Grilled Lemon Halibut

Marinade:
3 Tbsp. *each* low-sodium soy sauce
 and lemon juice
1 Tbsp. Worcestershire sauce
2 tsp. brown sugar
1 Tbsp. minced fresh ginger
 (*or* 1 tsp. ground)
1 clove garlic, minced

1¹/₂ lbs. halibut, shark, seabass *or*
 swordfish

Mix all marinade ingredients. Place fish in a 9" x 13" pan and pour marinade over. Turn to coat thoroughly with marinade. Cover and marinate, in refrigerator, for 1 hour.

Grill or barbecue, turning once, until fish flakes easily with a fork, about 4 to 5 minutes per side.

Serves 4

Per serving:	Calories	Fat (g)	Cholesterol (mg)	Fiber (g)	Sodium (mg)
	203	4	54	0	580

Halibut Jardinere

1 cup carrots, julienne
1 cup celery, julienne
1 small onion, sliced
1 tsp. olive oil
2 Tbsp. water *or* white wine

1 tsp. basil
¹/₂ tsp. thyme
¹/₄ tsp. Lite Salt™
¹/₄ tsp. black pepper
2 lbs. halibut steaks

In a non-stick skillet, saute carrots, celery and onion in olive oil until tender, about 5 minutes. Stir in water (or wine), herbs, salt and pepper. Simmer, covered, one minute. Place fish on vegetables. Cover and simmer until fish flakes easily with a fork, about 8 to 10 minutes per inch of thickness.

Serves 4 to 6

Per serving:	Calories	Fat (g)	Cholesterol (mg)	Fiber (g)	Sodium (mg)
	188	4	48	1	158

Halibut Provencal

2 halibut steaks, 6 oz. each
1 Tbsp. olive oil (or less)
1 tomato, cored and diced
1/2 cup sliced fresh mushrooms
1/4 cup *each* chopped onion and
   green pepper
1/3 cup dry white wine

1 Tbsp. chopped fresh parsley
1 clove garlic, minced
1/4 tsp. black pepper
1/8 tsp. salt
1/8 tsp. thyme
1 bay leaf

Saute halibut in oil until lightly browned. Add remaining ingredients. Bring to a boil, then simmer, covered, 10 to 15 minutes.

Remove fish and vegetables; keep warm. Cook liquid until reduced to about 1/4 cup. Pour over fish and vegetables and serve.

Serves 2

Per serving:	Calories	Fat (g)	Cholesterol (mg)	Fiber (g)	Sodium (mg)
	276	9	54	2	237

Fish a' la Orange

1¹/₂ lbs. fish fillets (orange roughy,
   halibut, sole, cod, etc.)

Sauce:
1/4 cup non-fat dry milk
2/3 cup fresh orange juice
1 Tbsp. liquid margarine
1¹/₂ Tbsp. unbleached flour
2 tsp. orange zest
1 tsp. tarragon

Place fish in a baking dish coated with cooking spray. Bake at 400° for 8 to 10 minutes per inch of thickness or until fish flakes easily with a fork.

Meanwhile, prepare Sauce. Stir non-fat dry milk into orange juice. Set aside. Melt margarine in a small saucepan. Stir in flour and cook 1 to 2 minutes or until bubbly. Remove from heat and add orange juice mixture, stirring until smooth. Return to low heat; cook and stir until thickened, 3 to 4 minutes. Add tarragon and orange zest. Serve over fish.

Serves 6

Per serving:	Calories	Fat (g)	Cholesterol (mg)	Fiber (g)	Sodium (mg)
	282	11	59	0	319

Orange Roughy with Lime-Curry Sauce

1/2 cup dry white wine
2 lbs. orange roughy fillets
1 cup plain non-fat yogurt
2 Tbsp. low-sugar orange marmalade

1 Tbsp. lime juice
1 tsp. curry powder
1 green onion, minced
1/4 cup toasted almond slices

Pour wine over fillets in a shallow casserole dish. Bake at 400° for 5 to 10 minutes or until fish flakes easily with a fork.

Meanwhile, blend remaining ingredients. Drain fish and serve with curry sauce. Garnish with almonds.

Serves 6 to 8

Per serving:	Calories	Fat (g)	Cholesterol (mg)	Fiber (g)	Sodium (mg)
	287	12	60	0	298

Steamed Salmon with Balsamic Glaze

1 lb. salmon fillets
Lettuce leaves
3 Tbsp. dark brown sugar

1 Tbsp. liquid margarine
1 to 2 tsp. Balsamic vinegar

Arrange salmon fillets on lettuce leaves and place in steamer basket. Set over boiling water in a skillet or wok; cover with lid. Steam for 8 to 10 minutes; fish is done when it flakes easily with a fork.

Combine brown sugar, margarine and Balsamic vinegar in a small saucepan. Cook over medium heat until well blended, 2 to 3 minutes. Serve sauce over steamed salmon.

Serves 4

Per serving:	Calories	Fat (g)	Cholesterol (mg)	Fiber (g)	Sodium (mg)
	275	12	68	0	107

Crusty BBQ Salmon

2 lbs. salmon fillets
2 lemons

2 Tbsp. brown sugar
1 tsp. tarragon

Rinse fish and pat dry. Lay on foil, then trim foil to fit fish. Squeeze lemon juice over fish then rub brown sugar through a strainer and sprinkle evenly all over salmon fillets. Sprinkle with tarragon.

Place on barbecue grill and cook over medium heat for 8 to 10 minutes per inch of thickness or until opaque in thickest part (cut to test; do not overcook).

Serves 6 to 8

Per serving:	Calories	Fat (g)	Cholesterol (mg)	Fiber (g)	Sodium (mg)
	225	9	68	0	68

Broiled Salmon with Yogurt Mustard Sauce

1 cup Yogurt Mustard Sauce (page 34)
1/2 cup thinly sliced green onion
1 lb. salmon fillets

Combine Mustard Sauce with green onions and set aside.

Broil salmon about 6" from broiler for 5 to 7 minutes. Turn fillets and spread generously with Mustard Sauce. Broil about 5 minutes longer or until fish flakes easily with a fork.

Yield: 4 servings

Per serving:	Calories	Fat (g)	Cholesterol (mg)	Fiber (g)	Sodium (mg)
	249	10	71	0	221

Herbed Salmon Fillets

1 lb. salmon fillets
1/4 cup *each* lemon juice and olive oil
2 green onions, thinly sliced

2 Tbsp. minced fresh parsley
1/4 tsp. rosemary
1/8 tsp. black pepper

Place salmon filets on heavy duty foil then trim foil to just fit.

Combine remaining ingredients, mixing well. Brush generously over salmon; let stand 30 minutes.

Barbecue salmon, basting often with remaining marinade. Cook, without turning, until fish is no longer pink in thickest part, 8 to 10 minutes per inch of thickness.

Serves 4

Per serving:	Calories	Fat (g)	Cholesterol (mg)	Fiber (g)	Sodium (mg)
	276	15	68	0	68

Salmon Oriental

1/2 cup orange juice
1 Tbsp. low-sodium soy sauce
2 Tbsp. catsup
2 Tbsp. chopped fresh parsley

1 Tbsp. lemon juice
1 clove garlic, minced
1 Tbsp. minced fresh ginger
1 1/2 lbs. salmon fillets

Mix together all ingredients, except fish. Place fish in 9" x 13" pan. Pour marinade over fish and marinate in refrigerator 1 hour (or more), turning fish 2 or 3 times.

Broil fish, basting with marinade.

Serves 6

Per serving:	Calories	Fat (g)	Cholesterol (mg)	Fiber (g)	Sodium (mg)
	229	9	68	0	220

Poached Salmon

1½ cups dry white wine
½ cup water
½ onion, sliced
½ lemon, sliced
4 sprigs parsley

1 bay leaf
4 peppercorns
1 stalk celery, including top, sliced
1 lb. salmon fillets (or other fish)
Tangy Dill Sauce (recipe follows)

Combine all ingredients except salmon in a skillet. Bring to a boil; reduce heat and simmer, uncovered, for 10 to 15 minutes.

Add salmon. Cover and simmer an additional 10 minutes or until fish flakes easily with a fork. Drain and serve immediately with Tangy Dill Sauce.

Note: A rule of thumb for poaching fish is to simmer 10 minutes per inch of thickness.

Serves 4

Per serving:	Calories	Fat (g)	Cholesterol (mg)	Fiber (g)	Sodium (mg)
	210	9	68	0	67

Tangy Dill Sauce

1 cup plain non-fat yogurt
2 Tbsp. sour cream
1 small cucumber, seeded and
    finely chopped

2 green onions, thinly sliced
½ clove garlic, minced
½ tsp. dill
½ tsp. lemon *or* lime juice

In a small bowl, combine all ingredients and blend well. Cover and chill before serving.

Yield: 2¼ cups; 1 serving = 2 Tbsp.

Per serving:	Calories	Fat (g)	Cholesterol (mg)	Fiber (g)	Sodium (mg)
	11	0	1	0	10

Salmon Loaf

1 onion, chopped
1/4 cup chopped celery, including tops
2 tsp. soft margarine *or* olive oil
2 cups whole wheat bread crumbs
1 15-oz. can salmon, drained and
   flaked
1 cup non-fat milk

1 Tbsp. lemon juice
2 Tbsp. minced fresh parsley
1 tsp. dill
Dash black pepper
1/2 tsp. Worcestershire sauce
3 egg whites

Saute onions and celery in oil until soft. Combine with remaining ingredients. Place in a 9" x 5" loaf pan coated with cooking spray. Bake, uncovered, at 425° for 45 minutes. Serve with Yogurt Mustard Sauce (page 34).

Serves 4 to 6

Per serving:	Calories	Fat (g)	Cholesterol (mg)	Fiber (g)	Sodium (mg)
	194	6	50	2	436

Salmon in Ginger Vinaigrette

This sauce is as versatile as it is flavorful. It is Oriental in inspiration, and the flavors of the cilantro, ginger, and sesame oil blend for a taste that is bright and clear, while not overly spicy.

1¹/₂ Tbsp. minced fresh ginger
3 shallots, minced
¹/₂ cup rice vinegar
Juice of 2 limes
2 Tbsp. low-sodium soy sauce
Black pepper to taste
Oriental sesame oil to taste (less than
   1 Tbsp.)

3/4 cup olive oil
1¹/₂ lbs. salmon fillets
1 bunch parsley *or* cilantro, chopped
2 Tbsp. sesame seeds, toasted in a
   350° oven for 10 minutes

Combine the ginger, shallots, vinegar, lime juice, soy sauce and pepper. Whisk in the sesame and olive oils, beating until thick.

Place salmon in a shallow baking dish. Add water to the dish so that salmon is halfway covered. Bake at 350° for 15 to 20 minutes or until fish feels firm to the touch.

Add parsley or cilantro to the dressing. Serve the salmon on 3 Tbsp. of the dressing, and garnish with the toasted sesame seeds.

Note: The sauce can be made in advance, but do not add the parsley or cilantro until the last minute or it will discolor.

Serves 6

Per serving:	Calories	Fat (g)	Cholesterol (mg)	Fiber (g)	Sodium (mg)
	289	16	68	0	513

Orange Sole

1 cup orange juice
1/2 cup dry white wine
1/4 tsp. *each* salt and pepper
2 carrots, julienne

1 zucchini, julienne
1 lb. sole fillets
2 Tbsp. chopped fresh cilantro, divided

Combine juice, wine, salt and pepper in a small saucepan and set aside.

Arrange vegetables on a dinner plate with a rim. Place on a rack in a large skillet. Pour 1/2 cup juice mixture over vegetables. Add 1/2" of water to skillet. Cover and steam 10 minutes. Add fish; cover and steam 8 minutes or more. Sprinkle with 1 Tbsp. cilantro.

Meanwhile, cook remaining juice mixture until reduced to 1/2 cup. Stir in remaining cilantro. Serve sauce over fish and vegetables.

Serves 4

Per serving:	Calories	Fat (g)	Cholesterol (mg)	Fiber (g)	Sodium (mg)
	179	2	44	1	247

Creole Snapper

1 lb. snapper fillets
1 Tbsp. olive oil
1 onion, chopped
1 green pepper, seeded and diced
1 red bell pepper, seeded and chopped
2 cloves garlic, minced
5 ripe tomatoes, cored and chopped *or*
   1 16-oz can salt-free tomatoes

1/4 cup chopped parsley
2 tsp. paprika
1/2 tsp. brown sugar
Dash Tabasco sauce
1 bay leaf
1 Tbsp. cornstarch
1 Tbsp. water
2 cups cooked brown rice

Cut snapper into chunks and set aside. Heat olive oil in a large skillet; saute onion, peppers and garlic until onion is soft, about 5 minutes. Add tomatoes, parsley, paprika, brown sugar, Tabasco and bay leaf. Simmer, covered, for 30 minutes.

Add snapper pieces; cook 5 to 8 minutes or until fish flakes easily with a fork. Blend together cornstarch and water. Add to sauce and cook, stirring, until thickened. Remove bay leaf and serve over rice.

Serves 4

Per serving:	Calories	Fat (g)	Cholesterol (mg)	Fiber (g)	Sodium (mg)
	352	6	76	5	387

Snapper in Tomato Wine Sauce

1/2 onion, sliced
1 cup sliced mushrooms
1 Tbsp. olive oil
1/2 cup salt-free tomato sauce

1/4 cup dry white wine
1/2 tsp. *each* oregano and basil
2 lbs. red snapper

Saute onion and mushrooms in oil. Add tomato sauce, wine, oregano and basil. Simmer 5 minutes. Pour over fish in a baking dish. Bake at 350° for 20 to 30 minutes or until fish flakes easily with a fork.

Serves 4 to 6

Per serving:	Calories	Fat (g)	Cholesterol (mg)	Fiber (g)	Sodium (mg)
	215	4	101	1	131

Swordfish Kebabs

1 lb. swordfish
2 Tbsp. olive oil
1 Tbsp. lemon juice
1 Tbsp. white wine vinegar

1 clove garlic, minced
2 bay leaves, crumbled
Pinch cayenne pepper

Remove skin from swordfish and cut into 1" cubes. Blend together remaining ingredients for marinade.

Place fish cubes in a 8" x 8" dish and pour marinade over, coating pieces evenly. Marinate at room temperature for one hour.

Thread fish on skewers and broil or grill until done, about 3 to 4 minutes per side. Brush with marinade while cooking. Serve with Creamy Cucumbers (page 41).

Variation: Alternate any of the following vegetables on the skewer: zucchini, yellow squash, mushrooms, cherry tomatoes, red or green peppers.

Serves 4

Per serving:	Calories	Fat (g)	Cholesterol (mg)	Fiber (g)	Sodium (mg)
	200	11	44	0	102

Tuna with Tomato Basil Sauce

2 lbs. tuna *or* grouper fillets
2 Tbsp. olive oil, divided
Black pepper
1 clove garlic, minced
3 large ripe tomatoes, chopped

1 red onion, chopped
1/4 cup lemon juice
1/4 tsp. *each* salt, black pepper and sugar
1/4 cup fresh basil, chopped

Brush tuna or grouper with oil; sprinkle with pepper. Grill or broil until fish flakes easily with a fork, about 8 to 10 minutes per inch of thickness.

Meanwhile, saute garlic, tomatoes, onion and lemon juice in remaining olive oil. Add salt, pepper and sugar. Cook until thickened, 10 to 15 minutes. Add basil. Serve over fish.

Serves 4 to 6

Per serving:	Calories	Fat (g)	Cholesterol (mg)	Fiber (g)	Sodium (mg)
	288	11	91	1	94

Baked Trout with Fresh Herbs

(from Marina Landing)

1 trout, boned, head on or off
1 Tbsp. chopped fresh parsley
1 1/2 tsp. chopped fresh basil *or*
  3/4 tsp. dried basil
1/2 tsp. chopped fresh oregano *or*
  1/4 tsp. dried oregano

1/4 tsp. chopped fresh thyme *or*
  pinch dried thyme
2 tsp. fresh lemon juice
1 tsp. olive oil
Pinch salt
Black pepper to taste

Lay the trout open, belly side up and sprinkle the herbs over the trout. Sprinkle the olive oil, salt and pepper over the herbs. Fold the trout and place in a 8" x 8" baking pan coated with cooking spray. Bake at 400° for 10 to 15 minutes, or until done (when it feels firm to the touch).

Remove the trout from the oven, place it on a plate and unfold it, so the herbs and meat are exposed.

Note: Trout may also be cooked on an outside grill.

Serves 1

Per serving:	Calories	Fat (g)	Cholesterol (mg)	Fiber (g)	Sodium (mg)
	249	10	96	1	48

Crispy Baked Fish

1 lb. fish fillets
1/4 tsp. Lite Salt™
Dash black pepper

1 Tbsp. olive *or* safflower oil
1/3 to 1/2 cup flaky whole grain cereal,
  crushed (e.g. bran flakes)

Wash and dry fish fillets; cut into serving pieces. Season with salt and pepper. Brush with oil and coat with crushed cereal.

Arrange in a single layer in a 8" x 8" baking dish coated with cooking spray. Bake at 500° for 10 minutes or until fish flakes easily with a fork.

Serves 4

Per serving:	Calories	Fat (g)	Cholesterol (mg)	Fiber (g)	Sodium (mg)
	271	13	58	0	439

Oven Poached Fish

1/4 cup chopped onion
1/2 cup *each* sliced mushrooms and
   chopped celery
1 lb. fish fillets

1 bay leaf
3 to 4 peppercorns
2 to 3 sprigs fresh parsley
1/4 cup *each* white wine and water

Spread onion, mushrooms and celery over bottom of a 8" x 8" baking dish coated with cooking spray. Place fish on top. Add seasonings, wine and water. Bake at 350° for 20 minutes or until fish flakes easily with a fork. Drain and serve immediately.

Serves 4

Per serving:	Calories	Fat (g)	Cholesterol (mg)	Fiber (g)	Sodium (mg)
	248	9	58	1	286

Greek Shellfish

1 Tbsp. olive oil
1 onion, chopped
1 28-oz. can crushed tomatoes
1/2 cup white wine
2 tsp. basil

1 tsp. oregano
1 lb. scallops
1/4 lb. uncooked shrimp, peeled
   and deveined
Black pepper

Heat olive oil in a large skillet. Saute onion until soft, about 5 minutes. Add tomatoes, wine, basil and oregano. Simmer, stirring occasionally, 10 to 15 minutes. Add scallops, shrimp and pepper to taste. Simmer 5 to 6 minutes or until done (do not overcook). Serve over brown rice.

Serves 4 to 5

Per serving:	Calories	Fat (g)	Cholesterol (mg)	Fiber (g)	Sodium (mg)
	216	5	82	4	515

Crab Foo Yung

1 egg
7 egg whites (about 1 cup)
1 7¹/2-oz. package bean sprouts,
  washed and drained
6 green onions, thinly sliced
1 6-oz. can crabmeat, rinsed,
  drained and flaked
¹/8 tsp. *each* black pepper and
  garlic powder
2 tsp. olive *or* safflower oil

Foo Yung Sauce:
1 tsp. *each* cornstarch and sugar
2 tsp. low-sodium soy sauce
1 tsp. vinegar
¹/2 cup salt-free chicken broth, defatted

Beat egg and whites together. Fold in sprouts, onions, crabmeat, pepper and garlic powder.

Heat oil in a large skillet. Drop ¹/4 cup egg mixture into pan and cook until set and lightly browned on bottom. Turn and brown other side. Keep warm while cooking remaining batter.

Foo Yung Sauce: In a saucepan combine cornstarch, sugar, soy sauce and vinegar. Stir in chicken broth. Cook over low heat, stirring constantly, until thickened. Serve over crab cakes.

Serves 4 to 6

Per serving:	Calories	Fat (g)	Cholesterol (mg)	Fiber (g)	Sodium (mg)
	151	6	95	1	568

Chicken

Turkey

Miscellaneous

Bombay Lime Chicken

(from The Canterbury Inn)

1/4 cup lime juice
4 green onions, thinly sliced
1/4 cup fresh mint, chopped
1/4 cup fresh cilantro, chopped
1 tsp. minced shallots

1 clove garlic, minced
1 tsp. black pepper
3/4 cup olive oil
4 chicken breasts, skinned

Combine all ingredients, except chicken breasts, and mix well. Pour marinade over chicken breasts and marinate for 1 hour.

Broil, brushing with marinade.

Serves 4

Per serving:	Calories	Fat (g)	Cholesterol (mg)	Fiber (g)	Sodium (mg)
	389	12	101	1	106

Nana's Chicken Cacciatore

2 lb. skinless, boneless chicken breasts
2 Tbsp. olive oil
1 onion, chopped
1 green pepper, seeded and chopped
1 clove garlic, minced
1 32-oz. cans Italian tomatoes,
    coarsely chopped

1 8-oz. can salt-free tomato sauce
2 Tbsp. chopped fresh parsley
1/2 tsp. thyme
1/2 lb. mushrooms, sliced
1/2 cup dry white wine

Saute chicken in oil until lightly browned. Remove; add onion, green pepper, and garlic. Saute until vegetables are soft. Add tomatoes, wine and chicken; simmer, covered, another 30 to 45 minutes. Remove cover for last 15 minutes to thicken sauce. Stir occasionally.

Serves 6 to 8

Per serving:	Calories	Fat (g)	Cholesterol (mg)	Fiber (g)	Sodium (mg)
	309	9	101	5	258

Hawaiian Honey Chicken

Marinade:

1 tsp. *each* lemon and orange zest
1/4 cup lemon juice
1/2 cup orange juice
2 Tbsp. honey

2 Tbsp. low-sodium soy sauce
1 tsp. dry mustard

6 chicken breast halves, skinned

Combine marinade ingredients and mix well. Add chicken pieces and coat evenly with marinade. Cover and marinate, stirring occasionally, for 2 to 4 hours.

Drain chicken. Bake chicken at 350° for about 45 minutes or until tender and cooked through. Baste occasionally with reduced marinade: in a one quart pan boil reserved marinade until reduced to about 1/3 cup.

Serves 6

Per serving:	Calories	Fat (g)	Cholesterol (mg)	Fiber (g)	Sodium (mg)
	256	5	101	0	298

Michael's Chicken

1/4 cup olive oil
1/4 cup Balsamic vinegar

1 Tbsp. Hidden Valley Ranch dressing mix
4 to 6 chicken breasts, skinned

Blend oil, vinegar and dressing mix. Pour over chicken, turning to coat evenly. Marinate 3 hours or overnight. Drain marinade, then grill chicken breasts until done.

Serves 4 to 6

Per serving:	Calories	Fat (g)	Cholesterol (mg)	Fiber (g)	Sodium (mg)
	309	14	101	0	368

Orange Teriyaki Chicken

1 6-oz. can frozen orange juice
  concentrate, thawed
1/4 cup low-sodium soy sauce
2 Tbsp. chopped onion

1/2 tsp. ground ginger (or 1 tsp. fresh)
1/2 tsp. hot pepper sauce
6 chicken breasts, skinned

Combine all ingredients but chicken. Add chicken, coating each piece with marinade. Cover and marinate 3 hours or more in refrigerator.

Remove from marinade and broil until chicken is tender and cooked through.

Serves 6

Per serving:	Calories	Fat (g)	Cholesterol (mg)	Fiber (g)	Sodium (mg)
	299	10	101	0	138

Mustard Marinated Chicken

Marinade:
1/2 cup dry white wine
1/2 cup olive oil
6 Tbsp. red wine vinegar
1/4 cup minced onion
2 cloves garlic, minced

1 tsp. thyme
1/2 tsp. black pepper
1/4 cup Dijon mustard

4 skinless, boneless chicken breasts

In a small bowl, whisk together wine, oil, vinegar, onion, garlic, thyme, pepper and mustard. Pour over chicken. Cover and refrigerate for 3 to 4 hours. (Pierce chicken with a fork to allow marinade to penetrate.)

Drain chicken and grill or broil until chicken is done. Baste frequently with marinade.

Serves 4

Per serving:	Calories	Fat (g)	Cholesterol (mg)	Fiber (g)	Sodium (mg)
	227	6	101	0	106

Honey-Mustard Glazed Chicken

1 Tbsp. olive *or* safflower oil
1/3 cup Dijon *or* Pommery mustard
2 Tbsp. honey

1 tsp. curry powder
1/2 tsp. tarragon
4 to 6 skinless, boneless chicken breasts

Blend oil, mustard, honey, curry powder and tarragon.

Arrange chicken in an 8" x 8" baking dish coated with cooking spray. Pour sauce over chicken. Bake at 350° for 15 to 20 minutes or until chicken is done.

Serves 4 to 6

Per serving:	Calories	Fat (g)	Cholesterol (mg)	Fiber (g)	Sodium (mg)
	269	8	101	0	270

Chicken Dijon

1/2 cup dry bread crumbs
1/4 cup Parmesan cheese
1 Tbsp. parsley
1/4 tsp. oregano

1/3 cup Dijon mustard
2 Tbsp. dry white wine
4 skinless, boneless chicken breasts

In a shallow dish or pan, combine bread crumbs, Parmesan, parsley and oregano. In another shallow dish, mix together mustard and wine.

Coat chicken in mustard mixture, then dip in bread crumbs. Place in an 8 inch square baking dish coated with cooking spray. Bake at 500° until golden brown and chicken is done in thickest part (cut to test), about 10 to 20 minutes.

Serves 4

Per serving:	Calories	Fat (g)	Cholesterol (mg)	Fiber (g)	Sodium (mg)
	308	8	107	0	488

Orange Apricot Chicken

1 cup dried apricots
1 1/2 cups orange juice
1 Tbsp. chopped fresh ginger
1 Tbsp. Oriental sesame oil
2 Tbsp. Dijon mustard

1 tsp. lemon zest
1 tsp. orange zest
1/4 tsp. ground cloves
6 chicken breasts, skinned

Soak apricots in juice until softened, about 1 hour. Combine all ingredients, except chicken, in a blender and puree until creamy. Marinate chicken in sauce overnight.

Bake chicken in marinade at 350° for 40 to 45 minutes or until done.

Serves 6

Per serving:	Calories	Fat (g)	Cholesterol (mg)	Fiber (g)	Sodium (mg)
	351	8	101	3	170

Chicken with Curried Fruit

1 Tbsp. olive oil
1 tsp. curry powder
4 skinless, boneless chicken breasts
2 Tbsp. dry sherry *or* vermouth
1/2 cup chopped (pitted) prunes
2 Tbsp. brown sugar

2 cups mixed fruit: peaches, pineapple,
  grapes, pears (your choice)
1 Tbsp. cornstarch
1 Tbsp. water
2 Tbsp. chopped cashews *or*
  toasted slivered almonds

Heat olive oil in a large skillet; add curry powder and saute briefly. Add chicken and saute until lightly browned. Stir in sherry and prunes. Bring to a boil, reduce heat, then simmer, covered, 10 to 15 minutes or until chicken is done (juices run clear when pierced with a fork in thickest part). Remove chicken to a plate.

Dissolve brown sugar in pan juices, then add fruit. Bring to a boil and cook until syrupy. Mix together cornstarch and water; stir into pan juices and cook, stirring, until thickened. Pour sauce over chicken; sprinkle with nuts and serve.

Serves 4

Per serving:	Calories	Fat (g)	Cholesterol (mg)	Fiber (g)	Sodium (mg)
	458	12	101	5	120

Tandoori Chicken

5 garlic cloves
2 Tbsp. minced fresh ginger
1 medium onion, cut into 8 wedges
1 cup plain non-fat yogurt
3 Tbsp. lemon *or* lime juice
1 Tbsp. olive oil
2 tsp. ground coriander
1 tsp. cumin
1 tsp. turmeric
1/2 tsp. black pepper

1/4 tsp. cardamom
1/4 tsp. nutmeg
1/4 tsp. ground cloves
1/4 tsp. cinnamon
1/4 tsp. cayenne pepper
8 skinless, boneless chicken breasts

Chopped green onion
Lemon wedges

Mince garlic, ginger and onion in food processor. Add next 12 ingredients and puree. Transfer to a large bowl. Cut deep slashes in chicken pieces. Add to marinade, turning to coat well. Cover. Refrigerate overnight.

Preheat broiler. Arrange chicken on broiler pan and broil about 3" from heat five minutes per side. Reduce oven temperature to 325°. Transfer chicken to baking dish coated with cooking spray. Bake until juices run clear when pierced with tip of sharp knife, basting frequently with marinade, 15 to 20 minutes. Garnish with green onion and lemon wedges.

Serves 4

Per serving:	Calories	Fat (g)	Cholesterol (mg)	Fiber (g)	Sodium (mg)
	364	7	103	0	121

Crispy Chicken

2 lbs. chicken parts, skinned
1 cup Rice Krispies™
1 tsp. chili powder
1/2 tsp. garlic powder

1/4 tsp. dry mustard
1/4 tsp. celery seed, crushed
1/4 tsp. paprika
1/2 cup Barbecue Sauce (recipe follows)

Rinse chicken; pat dry with paper towels. Mix together Rice Krispies and seasonings. Brush each chicken piece with barbecue sauce and roll in cereal mixture to coat.

Arrange chicken in a 9" x 13" baking pan coated with cooking spray. Bake, uncovered, at 375° for 50 minutes or until chicken is tender and coating is crisp. Do not turn.

Serves 6

Per serving:	Calories	Fat (g)	Cholesterol (mg)	Fiber (g)	Sodium (mg)
	331	11	130	0	193

Barbecue Sauce

2 cups salt-free tomato sauce
1/2 cup molasses
1/2 cup cider *or* white vinegar
1/2 cup brown sugar
1/4 cup olive *or* safflower oil

1/4 cup chopped onion
1 Tbsp. dry mustard
1 Tbsp. Worcestershire sauce
2 tsp. paprika
1/2 tsp. *each* black pepper and garlic powder

In a medium saucepan, bring all ingredients to a boil. Simmer, uncovered, for 30 minutes, stirring occasionally. Cool slightly, then pour into a jar, cover and store in refrigerator.

Yield: about 4 cups; 1 serving = 1/4 cup

Per serving:	Calories	Fat (g)	Cholesterol (mg)	Fiber (g)	Sodium (mg)
	195	7	0	1	39

Oven Fried Chicken

1 cup Oat Flour (recipe follows)
2 Tbsp. Parmesan cheese
1/2 tsp. *each* paprika and sage
1/2 tsp. herb seasoning (salt free)
1/4 tsp. black pepper

3 lbs. chicken pieces, skinned
2 egg whites
1/4 cup non-fat milk
1 Tbsp. liquid margarine

Combine first five ingredients and coat chicken with mixture. Beat egg whites and milk together; dip coated chicken into milk mixture, then coat again with dry ingredients.

Arrange chicken pieces in a 9" x 13" baking dish coated with cooking spray, then drizzle with margarine. Bake at 400° for 40 to 50 minutes or until tender and golden brown.

Serves 6 to 8

Per serving:	Calories	Fat (g)	Cholesterol (mg)	Fiber (g)	Sodium (mg)
	355	13	132	2	189

Oat Flour

1 1/4 cups rolled oats

Process oats in food processor or blender for about one minute.

Use for baking, breading or thickening. To use in baking, substitute up to one-third of the flour with oat flour.

Yield: 1 cup; 1 serving = 1/4 cup

Per serving:	Calories	Fat (g)	Cholesterol (mg)	Fiber (g)	Sodium (mg)
	78	1	0	3	1

Parmesan Chicken

(from "Crimes of Passion in the Kitchen")

Marinade:
1/2 cup plain non-fat yogurt
3 Tbsp. lemon juice
1 Tbsp. Dijon mustard
2 cloves garlic, minced
1/2 tsp. oregano
1/2 tsp. sage
6 chicken breast halves, skinned and boned

Coating:
1/2 cup dry breadcrumbs
2 Tbsp. Parmesan cheese
1 Tbsp. liquid margarine

Combine marinade ingredients. Pour over chicken, coating each piece. Marinate, covered, 2 hours or overnight in refrigerator.

Combine coating ingredients in a plastic bag or shallow bowl. Drain chicken and coat with breadcrumb mixture. Place in a baking dish coated with cooking spray and chill for one hour. Drizzle chicken with margarine and bake, uncovered, at 350° for 30 to 45 minutes or until tender and golden brown.

Serves 6

Per serving:	Calories	Fat (g)	Cholesterol (mg)	Fiber (g)	Sodium (mg)
	301	9	107	0	262

Spicy Chicken with Peanuts

2 skinless, boneless chicken breasts
2 tsp. olive *or* safflower oil
1 1/2" slice fresh ginger, minced
1 clove garlic, minced
1/4 to 1/2 tsp. dried chile pepper (optional)
1/4 cup dry roasted, unsalted peanuts
1 green pepper, seeded and sliced
1 onion, sliced

4 green onions, sliced in 1" pieces
3 stalks celery, sliced on the diagonal
1 cup sliced mushrooms
2 cups pre-cooked* chopped broccoli
1 cup pre-cooked* sliced carrots
2 cups snow peas
1 Tbsp. low-sodium soy sauce
1 tsp. Oriental sesame oil

Cut chicken into bite-size pieces. Heat wok or skillet. Add 1 tsp. oil; swirl to coat entire surface. Add ginger, garlic and chile pepper. Stir-fry one minute. (Avoid breathing chile fumes.) Add chicken and peanuts; stir-fry 2 to 3 minutes or until chicken is done. Remove and drain on paper towels.

Add remaining teaspoon of oil. Stir-fry remaining vegetables (except pea pods) until tender crisp. Add small amounts of water as needed to prevent sticking.

Add chicken, pea pods and soy sauce. Stir-fry one minute. Drizzle in sesame oil. Serve over steamed brown rice.

* To pre-cook, place chopped vegetables in plastic bag. Microwave 1 minute.

Variations:

•Other vegetables to add to the stir-fry are: zucchini, red or green cabbage, bok choy, water chestnuts, bamboo shoots, bean sprouts (add along with chicken at last minute)

•After vegetables are stir-fried, add 1 to 2 cups cooked brown rice. Stir-fry until rice is heated then add chicken, pea pods and seasonings.

•Substitute lean beef, scallops, orange roughy, monkfish, halibut, salmon or other firm white fish for chicken.

Serves 6 to 8

Per serving:	Calories	Fat (g)	Cholesterol (mg)	Fiber (g)	Sodium (mg)
	173	7	25	5	175

Roast Chicken

1 roasting chicken, skinned and excess
   fat removed
3 Tbsp. vinegar
3 Tbsp. olive oil

1 Tbsp. lemon juice
1/2 tsp. *each* savory, sage and basil
1 clove garlic, minced
12 oz. fresh mushrooms

In a small saucepan mix all ingredients except chicken and mushrooms. Bring sauce to a boil, stirring. Remove from heat. Dip mushrooms in sauce and set aside.

Brush chicken evenly with remaining sauce.

Place chicken on a rack in roasting pan. Roast at 375°, basting every 20 minutes, for 1 to 1¹/₂ hours or until chicken is done. Add mushrooms to pan during last 20 minutes.

Serves 4

Per serving:	Calories	Fat (g)	Cholesterol (mg)	Fiber (g)	Sodium (mg)
	326	18	97	4	106

Sage Vinaigrette

(from the Augusta in the Westin Hotel)

2 Tbsp. sherry vinegar
1¹/₂ Tbsp. Dijon mustard
1 Tbsp. chopped fresh sage *or*
   1 tsp. dried sage
1 cup olive oil

Blend vinegar, mustard and sage in a blender or food processor. Slowly drizzle in oil with motor running until all is incorporated. Heat gently in a double boiler before serving.

Especially good with chicken. Use sparingly as this sauce is quite high in fat.

Yield: about 1¹/₄ cups; 1 serving = 2 Tbsp.

Per serving:	Calories	Fat (g)	Cholesterol (mg)	Fiber (g)	Sodium (mg)
	161	18	0	0	24

Turkey Picatta

1 lb. turkey cutlets
3 egg whites, lightly beaten
1 Tbsp. (or less) olive oil
2 tsp. cornstarch

1/2 cup salt-free chicken broth, defatted
1 lemon, cut in half
1 Tbsp. capers, rinsed and drained

Dip cutlets into egg whites. Saute in olive oil until golden brown, 2 to 3 minutes on each side. Remove from pan and keep warm.

Blend cornstarch into chicken broth. Pour into skillet. Cook and stir until thickened. Squeeze in juice of 1/2 lemon. Add capers. Cook 1 to 2 minutes until warmed through. Pour sauce over turkey cutlets and serve.

Serves 4

Per serving:	Calories	Fat (g)	Cholesterol (mg)	Fiber (g)	Sodium (mg)
	250	8	85	0	149

Orange-Tarragon Turkey Cutlets

1/4 cup unbleached flour
1/2 tsp. tarragon, crumbled
1 1/2 lbs. turkey slices
1 Tbsp. olive oil

1/4 cup chopped shallots *or* green onions
1 cup fresh orange juice
1/3 cup dry white wine
1 Tbsp. orange zest

Combine flour and tarragon in a plastic bag. Add turkey slices a few at a time and shake until well coated.

Heat olive oil in a large skillet. Add one-half of the turkey slices and cook until lightly browned, 1 to 2 minutes per side. Remove to a serving dish and keep warm. Repeat with remaining turkey. (If skillet is dry, coat with cooking spray.)

Add shallots to pan and saute 2 minutes. Add orange juice, wine and zest. Boil over high heat until mixture is reduced by one-half. Reduce heat to low; add turkey slices and coat thoroughly with sauce. Serve warm.

Serves 6

Per serving:	Calories	Fat (g)	Cholesterol (mg)	Fiber (g)	Sodium (mg)
	271	7	85	0	95

Turkey Stroganoff

1 lb. ground turkey
1 onion, chopped
1 lb. mushrooms, sliced
1/4 cup dry sherry *or* white wine
Dash nutmeg

1 cup 1% cottage cheese
1/2 cup plain non-fat yogurt
1 Tbsp. lemon juice
8 oz. eggless noodles *or* fettuccine

Coat a non-stick pan with cooking spray. Add ground turkey, onion and mushrooms. Saute until turkey is no longer pink. Add sherry and nutmeg. Simmer for 15 minutes.

In a food processor or blender, puree cottage cheese, yogurt and lemon juice until smooth. Add to turkey and stir until heated through (do not boil). Serve over noodles.

Serves 4 to 6

Per serving:	Calories	Fat (g)	Cholesterol (mg)	Fiber (g)	Sodium (mg)
	308	4	52	4	236

Turkey Loaf

(from Jane Brody's "Good Food Book")

2 cloves garlic, minced
1 cup chopped celery, including tops
1 cup thinly sliced leeks *or*
  1/2 cup chopped onion
1 1/2 cup diced red bell pepper
1 Tbsp. safflower *or* olive oil
2 1/2 cups sliced mushrooms (1/2 lb.)

1 1/4 lbs. ground turkey
2 egg whites
1/2 tsp. black pepper
Dash nutmeg
1 slice whole wheat bread, diced
1/2 cup minced fresh parsley

In a large skillet saute garlic, celery, leeks (or onion) and red bell pepper in oil until vegetables are soft, about 3 to 5 minutes. Add mushrooms and continue cooking until liquid has evaporated. Stir frequently.

Meanwhile, in a large bowl combine turkey, egg whites, pepper, nutmeg, bread and parsley. Add sauteed vegetables and mix well. Transfer mixture to a 9" x 5" loaf pan coated with cooking spray.

Place pan in a large, shallow baking dish. Pour boiling water into the outer pan to a depth of about one inch. Bake at 375° for 1 hour and 15 minutes. Let it rest in pan for 15 minutes then remove. Slice and serve. Delicious hot or cold.

Serves 8

Per serving:	Calories	Fat (g)	Cholesterol (mg)	Fiber (g)	Sodium (mg)
	133	4	46	3	102

Mexican Pita Tacos

1/2 lb. ground turkey *or* lean ground beef
1/2 cup chopped onion
1 clove garlic, minced
2 cups salt-free canned kidney beans
1/2 cup Mexican Salsa (page 5)

3 whole wheat pita breads, halved
2 cups shredded lettuce
1 tomato, cored and diced
1 cup (4 oz.) grated part-skim
  mozzarella cheese

Brown ground turkey with onion and garlic; drain if necessary. Add kidney beans and Mexican Salsa; simmer 5 to 10 minutes.

Spoon 1/2 cup mixture into each pita half. Top with lettuce, tomato and cheese. Add additional Salsa if desired.

Serves 6

Per serving:	Calories	Fat (g)	Cholesterol (mg)	Fiber (g)	Sodium (mg)
	209	4	20	9	108

Chili Con Carne

1 cup chopped onions
1 clove garlic, minced
1 tsp. olive oil
2 lbs. ground turkey *or* lean ground beef
2 to 4 tsp. chili powder
2 tsp. cumin
1 tsp. *each* oregano and paprika
1/4 tsp. *each* cayenne pepper and
  black pepper

1/4 tsp. salt
1 14 1/2-oz. can salt-free, defatted
  chicken broth
1 28-oz. can salt-free crushed tomatoes,
  undrained
2 15-oz. cans salt-free kidney beans,
  undrained

Saute onions and garlic in olive oil until tender. Add turkey and continue cooking until crumbly and browned. Add seasonings, broth and tomatoes. Simmer, covered, for 30 minutes stirring occasionally. Add beans and simmer 10 to 15 minutes more.

Serves 8 to 10

Per serving:	Calories	Fat (g)	Cholesterol (mg)	Fiber (g)	Sodium (mg)
	232	4	59	10	199

Turkey Curry

1 onion, chopped
1/2 cup diced red bell pepper
1 to 2 tsp. olive oil
1 lb. ground turkey
1 cup chopped celery

1 to 2 tsp. curry powder
1 1/2 cups salt-free chicken broth, defatted
1 1/2 Tbsp. cornstarch
1 Tbsp. lemon juice

In a large skillet, saute onion and red bell pepper in olive oil until soft. Add ground turkey, celery and curry powder, and cook, stirring, until turkey loses its pink color.

Blend 2 Tbsp. broth with cornstarch to make a paste. Pour remaining broth into skillet and bring to a boil. Add cornstarch; cook and stir until thickened. Stir in lemon juice.

Serve over brown rice accompanied by assorted condiments:

•raisins

•chopped, unsalted, dry roasted peanuts or cashews

•chopped, unpeeled (seeded) cucumber

•pineapple tidbits (juice packed)

Serves 6

Per serving:	Calories	Fat (g)	Cholesterol (mg)	Fiber (g)	Sodium (mg)
	223	6	98	1	131

Lemon-Sesame Asparagus

2 Tbsp. rice vinegar
1 Tbsp. water
2 tsp. Oriental sesame oil
2 tsp. lemon juice

1 tsp. lemon zest
1 1/2 tsp. sesame seeds, toasted
1 1/2 lbs. fresh asparagus, trimmed

In a small bowl, combine vinegar, water, sesame oil, lemon juice and zest; mix well. Steam asparagus until tender-crisp, 4 to 6 minutes. Remove to a serving dish. Pour dressing over asparagus and sprinkle with sesame seeds.

Serves 6 to 8

Per serving:	Calories	Fat (g)	Cholesterol (mg)	Fiber (g)	Sodium (mg)
	32	2	0	1	163

Dill Green Beans

1/2 lb. fresh green beans
2 Tbsp. dill seed
1 1/2 cups water
1/2 cup red wine vinegar
2 Tbsp. sugar

1 clove garlic, minced
1/2 tsp. celery seed
1/4 tsp. crushed red pepper flakes
1/2 cup sliced onion rings

Trim ends from green beans and cut in 2" pieces. Place dill seed in a small bowl and crush with a spoon.

In a medium saucepan combine all ingredients except green beans and onion. Bring to a boil. Reduce heat and simmer, covered, 5 minutes. Add green beans and onions; simmer until beans are just tender, 2 to 3 minutes.

Pour into a tightly covered container and chill before serving. Add to a tossed salad or serve as an appetizer.

Serves 4 to 6

Per serving:	Calories	Fat (g)	Cholesterol (mg)	Fiber (g)	Sodium (mg)
	35	0	0	1	4

Carrots with Balsamic Glaze

6 carrots, sliced
1 Tbsp. liquid margarine

3 Tbsp. dark brown sugar
1 to 2 tsp. Balsamic vinegar

Steam carrots until tender-crisp. Meanwhile, combine margarine, brown sugar and Balsamic vinegar in a small saucepan. Cook over medium heat until well blended, 2 to 3 minutes. Combine sauce with steamed carrots and serve.

Variation: Add steamed snow peas.

Serves 4 to 6

Per serving:	Calories	Fat (g)	Cholesterol (mg)	Fiber (g)	Sodium (mg)
	73	2	0	1	62

Confetti Corn

1 green *or* red bell pepper, chopped
1 onion, chopped
1 tsp. olive oil

1 10-oz. pkg. frozen corn, cooked
1 tomato, cored and chopped

Saute pepper and onion in oil until soft. Add corn and tomato. Cover; cook 1 to 2 minutes or until heated through.

Serves 3 to 4

Per serving:	Calories	Fat (g)	Cholesterol (mg)	Fiber (g)	Sodium (mg)
	98	1	0	4	8

Corn Cakes

1 8-oz. can salt-free corn, well drained　　**2 egg whites**
1/4 cup non-fat milk　　**1/4 cup whole wheat flour**

Mix corn, milk and egg whites in blender or food processor until a chunky paste forms. Mix in flour.

Coat a non-stick pan or griddle with cooking spray. Drop batter by tablespoonfuls and cook over medium heat until pancakes are golden brown and set, about 2 to 3 minutes per side.

Yield: about 6 to 8; 1 serving = 2 corn cakes

Per serving:	Calories	Fat (g)	Cholesterol (mg)	Fiber (g)	Sodium (mg)
	80	3	0	2	33

Crispy Potato Skins

2 baking potatoes, scrubbed　　**1/4 tsp _each_ garlic powder and salt**
1/2 tsp. onion powder　　**2 tsp. olive _or_ safflower oil**

Bake potatoes. Slice each in half and scoop out insides leaving about 1/4" potato on skin. (Reserve potato for another use.) Combine seasonings and sprinkle over potato. Drizzle with oil and mix well.

Bake at 300° on a non-stick baking sheet for 20 to 30 minutes or until crisp. Serve with HealthMark Sour Cream (page 3) or other topping, if desired.

Optional: Sprinkle with 1 Tbsp. Parmesan cheese before baking.

Serves 2 to 4

Per serving:	Calories	Fat (g)	Cholesterol (mg)	Fiber (g)	Sodium (mg)
	67	2	0	1	135

Oven Fried Potatoes

2 baking potatoes, scrubbed
2 tsp. olive *or* safflower oil

¹/₄ tsp. *each* salt, black pepper and garlic powder
¹/₂ tsp. paprika

Slice potatoes into thin strips as for french fries. Toss with oil in a medium bowl. Combine seasonings and sprinkle over potato strips, mixing well.

Spread on non-stick baking sheet. Bake at 350° for 20 to 30 minutes or until browned.

Variation: Eliminate above seasonings. Sprinkle with Herb Salt before baking.

Herb Salt:
1 tsp. Lite Salt™
2 to 3 tsp. garlic powder
2 tsp. paprika
1 to 2 tsp. chili powder

1 tsp. *each* turmeric and black pepper
¹/₂ tsp. *each* ground ginger, dry mustard, celery seed, onion powder and dill

Serves 2 to 4

Per serving:	Calories	Fat (g)	Cholesterol (mg)	Fiber (g)	Sodium (mg)
	67	2	0	1	135

Stuffed Baked Potato

6 potatoes, baked
1¹/₂ cups HealthMark Sour Cream
  (page 3)

4 green onions, thinly sliced
6 tsp. Parmesan cheese
Paprika

Scoop pulp out of potatoes. Mash and mix with HealthMark Sour Cream and green onions. Spoon back into potato shells, mounding slightly. Dust tops with cheese and paprika. Bake at 425° until lightly browned, 5 to 10 minutes.

Serves 6

Per serving:	Calories	Fat (g)	Cholesterol (mg)	Fiber (g)	Sodium (mg)
	151	2	7	1	234

Maple Glazed Sweet Potatoes

1/2 cup orange juice
1 Tbsp. cornstarch
1/2 cup maple syrup
1 Tbsp. orange zest

1 cinnamon stick
6 cloves
1 1/2 lbs. sweet potatoes,
    cooked and quartered

In a small bowl, blend orange juice into cornstarch. Pour into a large skillet; add maple syrup, orange zest, cinnamon stick and cloves. Cook over medium heat, stirring, until thickened and clear. Add sweet potatoes and heat through. Remove cinnamon stick and cloves before serving.

Serves 6 to 8

Per serving:	Calories	Fat (g)	Cholesterol (mg)	Fiber (g)	Sodium (mg)
	151	0	0	0	13

Ratatouille

2 cloves garlic, minced
2 onions, thinly sliced
1 to 2 Tbsp. olive oil
2 green *and/or* red bell peppers, julienne
2 zucchini, sliced

1 unpeeled eggplant, chopped
4 ripe tomatoes, cored and chopped
1/2 tsp. *each* salt, black pepper, oregano and basil
1/4 tsp. thyme
2 Tbsp. chopped fresh parsley

Saute garlic and onion in oil until soft. Stir in peppers, zucchini and eggplant. Continue cooking for 5 minutes, stirring occasionally. Add tomatoes and seasonings. Cover and simmer 20 to 30 minutes, stirring occasionally. Uncover and cook over low heat for 10 to 15 minutes or until liquid evaporates.

Serves 8

Per serving:	Calories	Fat (g)	Cholesterol (mg)	Fiber (g)	Sodium (mg)
	69	2	0	3	144

Mustard Glazed Sprouts

4 cups Brussels sprouts, trimmed
2 Tbsp. cider *or* Balsamic vinegar
3 Tbsp. brown sugar

1 to 2 Tbsp. Dijon mustard
1 Tbsp. liquid margarine

Steam Brussels sprouts until tender when pierced with a fork, about 15 to 20 minutes.

Meanwhile, in a medium skillet, combine remaining ingredients over medium heat and cook until bubbling. Add cooked sprouts and stir until well coated with glaze.

Serves 4

Per serving:	Calories	Fat (g)	Cholesterol (mg)	Fiber (g)	Sodium (mg)
	132	4	0	5	154

Creamed Spinach

Delicious as a baked potato topping

1 cup White Sauce (page 155)
1 10-oz. pkg. frozen chopped spinach,
  thawed and drained *or*
2 cups chopped fresh spinach

1/4 tsp. nutmeg *or* tarragon
1/4 tsp. Lite Salt™

In a medium saucepan, combine all ingredients. Simmer until warm.

Variation: Substitute chopped cooked broccoli for spinach.

Serves 6

Per serving:	Calories	Fat (g)	Cholesterol (mg)	Fiber (g)	Sodium (mg)
	79	3	2	1	152

White (Bechamel) Sauce

This low fat version of a classic white sauce can be the start of many interesting sauces and soups

1 cup non-fat milk
1/4 cup non-fat dry milk
1 1/2 Tbsp. liquid margarine

2 Tbsp. unbleached flour
1/4 tsp. white pepper

Combine liquid and dry milk; mix well to dissolve powdered milk. Set aside.

In a small saucepan, melt margarine. Stir in flour and cook for 1 minute. Do not brown. Remove from heat and gradually whisk in milk mixture. Add pepper. Cook and stir over medium heat until thickened.

Tip: For a subtle herb flavor, combine 1 bay leaf, 2 peppercorns, 1 slice onion and 2 sprigs parsley with milk mixture; cover and refrigerate overnight to infuse flavors. Strain before using.

Per serving:	Serving size	Calories	Fat (g)	Cholesterol (mg)	Fiber (g)	Sodium (mg)
	2 Tbsp	82	4	2	0	102

Variations:

• Cheese Sauce:
3/4 cup grated part-skim mozzarella
  (*or* other low-fat) cheese

1/4 tsp. dry mustard *or* nutmeg
1/4 tsp. paprika

Add above to cooked sauce and stir until cheese melts.

• Curry Sauce:
1/2 to 1 tsp. curry powder
1/4 tsp. dry mustard
1/4 tsp. paprika

Stir into sauce along with milk.

• Parmesan Sauce:
1/3 cup Parmesan cheese
1 clove garlic, finely minced
1/4 tsp. nutmeg
1/4 tsp. white pepper

Add above to cooked sauce and stir until cheese melts.

• Sherry Mushroom Sauce — Add 1/2 cup finely diced mushrooms and 2 Tbsp. dry sherry along with milk.

• Veloute Sauce — Substitute 1 cup salt-free chicken broth (defatted) for 1 cup non-fat milk.

Yield: 1 1/4 cups

Tomatoes Florentine

2 Tbsp. chopped onion
2 Tbsp. chopped fresh parsley
1/2 tsp. savory
1 1/2 cups cooked chopped spinach,
   drained well

3 ripe tomatoes, halved and seeded
2 Tbsp. seasoned bread crumbs
1 Tbsp. Parmesan cheese

Combine onion, parsley, savory and spinach. Stuff tomatoes with spinach mixture. Mix bread crumbs with cheese and spread on top of tomatoes. Bake at 375° for 15 minutes.

Serves 6

Per serving:	Calories	Fat (g)	Cholesterol (mg)	Fiber (g)	Sodium (mg)
	36	1	1	2	50

Zucchini Saute

1 to 2 tsp. olive oil
4 zucchini, julienne
1 green *or* red bell pepper, julienne
1 clove garlic, minced

1 tsp. *each* basil and oregano
1 Tbsp. chopped fresh parsley
Black pepper to taste

Heat oil in large skillet (non-stick preferred). Stir-fry zucchini, green peppers and garlic until tender-crisp, about 3 to 4 minutes. Sprinkle with herbs and pepper.

Serves 4 to 6

Per serving:	Calories	Fat (g)	Cholesterol (mg)	Fiber (g)	Sodium (mg)
	40	2	0	0	2

Zucchini Flan

6 small zucchini, sliced
1 cup evaporated non-fat milk
5 egg whites

2 Tbsp. Parmesan cheese
1/4 tsp. *each* black pepper, paprika
  and garlic powder

Steam zucchini until tender-crisp. Place in a 1 1/2 quart baking dish coated with cooking spray.

Beat together remaining ingredients and pour over zucchini. Sprinkle with additional paprika. Bake at 325° for 30 to 40 minutes or until knife inserted into center comes out clean.

Serves 6

Per serving:	Calories	Fat (g)	Cholesterol (mg)	Fiber (g)	Sodium (mg)
	92	2	6	1	132

Tortilla Packets

1 10-oz. pkg. frozen chopped spinach,
  thawed
4 flour tortillas (made with soy oil)

8 oz. part-skim mozzarella cheese, sliced
4 cloves garlic, minced
1/2 cup Marinara Sauce (page 87)

Squeeze moisture from spinach; set aside.

Arrange tortillas in a single layer on a baking pan; coat lightly with cooking spray. Place in a 500° oven for 20 to 30 seconds or until warm and pliable. Turn tortillas over and layer equal portions of spinach, cheese and garlic in center of each. Fold in sides to form a packet and place seam side down on baking sheet. Coat lightly with cooking spray. Bake at 450° for 6 to 7 minutes or until tortillas brown lightly around the edges.

Meanwhile, heat Marinara Sauce. Place tortilla packets on plate and serve with Marinara Sauce spooned over the top.

Serves 4

Per serving:	Calories	Fat (g)	Cholesterol (mg)	Fiber (g)	Sodium (mg)
	296	11	32	2	722

Baked Potato Toppings

Instead of the usual high-fat toppings try:

- HealthMark Sour Cream (page 3). Add 1 Tbsp. chives or thinly sliced green onion
- Plain non-fat yogurt mixed with mustard, chives, chopped green onion, dill, parsley, oregano, basil or horseradish
- Chive-yogurt topping: combine 1 cup plain non-fat yogurt, 2 Tbsp. chives or chopped green onion, 1 Tbsp. lemon juice, 1 tsp. lemon zest and 1 clove garlic, minced
- Mustard
- Lemon juice
- Balsamic or other flavored vinegar (a teaspoon or so will be enough)
- Barbecue sauce, low-sodium catsup; cocktail sauce (just a spoonful or so)
- 1% cottage cheese
- A few drops *each* Oriental sesame oil and low-sodium soy sauce
- Salsa
- Guacamole
- Vegetarian baked beans or vegetarian chili
- 1 Tbsp. Parmesan cheese
- Ranch Dressing (page 29)

Cooking for a Healthier Ever After

Apricot Bites

1/3 cup soft margarine
2 egg whites
1 cup chopped dried apricots
1/2 cup brown sugar
1/4 cup unbleached flour

2 cups bite-size shredded wheat squares,
  coarsely crushed
1/4 cup chopped walnuts
1/4 tsp. almond extract

Place margarine in a 2 1/2 quart bowl. Cook, uncovered, in microwave oven on HIGH 30 seconds to 1 minute, or until melted. Add egg whites, apricots, sugar and flour; stir until well combined.

Micro-cook, uncovered, 3 1/2 to 4 1/2 minutes, or until very thick, stirring every minute. Remove bowl from microwave. Cool apricot mixture about 5 minutes. Add crushed shredded wheat squares, chopped walnuts, and almond extract; stir until well combined. Shape into 1" balls. Store tightly covered in refrigerator.

Yield: about 40 pieces; 1 serving = 2 pieces

Per serving:	Calories	Fat (g)	Cholesterol (mg)	Fiber (g)	Sodium (mg)
	99	4	0	1	48

Apricot Oat Bars

3 Tbsp. soft margarine
3 Tbsp. *each* brown sugar and honey
1 1/2 cups rolled oats
2 Tbsp. whole wheat flour
2/3 cup chopped dried apricots
1/2 cup boiling water

2 egg whites
1/4 cup *each* brown sugar, whole wheat
  flour and oat bran
1 tsp. cinnamon
1/4 tsp. *each* nutmeg and cloves
1/3 cup chopped walnuts

Cream margarine with sugar and honey, then stir in oatmeal and whole wheat flour. Press into bottom of an 8" x 8" baking pan coated with cooking spray. Bake at 350° for 5 minutes.

Meanwhile combine apricots and boiling water; let stand for 10 minutes. Stir in egg whites, sugar, flour, oat bran and spices. Mix well, then stir in nuts. Spread evenly over baked layer. Bake at 350° for another 25 minutes. Cool; cut into squares.

Yield: 16 bars; 1 serving = 1 bar

Per serving:	Calories	Fat (g)	Cholesterol (mg)	Fiber (g)	Sodium (mg)
	116	4	0	2	37

Jubilation Cookies

(from The Gourmet Affair)

1/2 cup canola *or* safflower oil
1 cup honey
4 egg whites
2 tsp. vanilla
1/4 cup *each* sunflower and sesame seeds
1/2 cup raisins
1/2 cup chopped dried apricots

1/2 cup chopped walnuts *or* pecans
1 1/2 cups wheat germ *or* 1 cup wheat germ
    plus 1/2 cup oat bran
2 cups rolled oats
1 tsp. cinnamon
3/4 cup whole wheat flour
1/2 cup non-fat dry milk

Combine oil, honey, egg whites, vanilla, seeds, fruit, nuts, wheat germ, oatmeal and cinnamon. Let stand 15 minutes for oatmeal to soften.

Combine flour and dry milk. Add to oatmeal mixture and mix thoroughly. Add more flour if dough is sticky.

Drop cookies 1" apart on a non-stick cookie sheet. Bake at 375° for 10 to 12 minutes. Remove to a rack to cool.

Yield: 4 dozen; 1 serving = 1 cookie

Per serving:	Calories	Fat (g)	Cholesterol (mg)	Fiber (g)	Sodium (mg)
	102	4	0	1	12

Ellie's Brownies

10 Tbsp. canola oil
3/4 cup sugar (brown or white)
3 egg whites
1 Tbsp. vanilla

1/4 cup chocolate syrup
10 Tbsp. cocoa powder
1 cup unbleached flour
1 tsp. baking powder

In a medium bowl, beat together oil, sugar, egg whites, vanilla and chocolate syrup. Add cocoa powder, flour and baking powder. Beat until well blended.

Spread evenly in an 8" square baking dish coated with cooking spray. Bake at 350° for 20 minutes (do not overbake). Cool, then cut into squares.

Yield: 16 squares; 1 serving = 1 square

Per serving:	Calories	Fat (g)	Cholesterol (mg)	Fiber (g)	Sodium (mg)
	170	9	0	0	58

Cocoa Kisses

3 egg whites, at room temperature
1/2 tsp. cream of tartar

1/2 cup white sugar
2 Tbsp. cocoa powder

Beat egg whites until foamy. Add cream of tartar and beat until soft peaks form. Gradually beat in sugar a few tablespoons at a time. Beat until stiff. Fold in cocoa.

Drop batter by level tablespoonfuls on non-stick cookie sheets which have been sprayed with cooking spray. Bake at 275° for 18 to 20 minutes. Cool completely before removing from cookie sheet.

Yield: 8 dozen; 1 serving = 1 cookie

Per serving:	Calories	Fat (g)	Cholesterol (mg)	Fiber (g)	Sodium (mg)
	9	0	0	0	4

Molasses Cookies

3/4 cup canola *or* safflower oil
3/4 cup brown sugar
1/4 cup molasses
2 egg whites

2 tsp. baking soda
2 cups whole wheat flour
1 tsp. cinnamon
1/2 tsp. *each* cloves and ginger

Beat together oil, sugar, molasses and egg whites. Add remaining ingredients and blend well. Chill.

Form into 1" balls and place on a non-stick cookie sheet. Bake at 325° for 8 to 10 minutes. Remove from cookie sheet immediately and cool on a wire rack.

Yield: about 3 dozen; 1 serving = 1 cookie

Per serving:	Calories	Fat (g)	Cholesterol (mg)	Fiber (g)	Sodium (mg)
	86	5	0	1	50

Molasses Oat Chews

3/4 cup soft margarine
1/4 cup molasses
3/4 cup brown sugar
2 egg whites
1/2 tsp. *each* ginger and cloves

1 tsp. baking soda
13/4 cup whole wheat flour
3/4 cup rolled oats
1/2 cup oat bran

Cream together margarine, molasses and brown sugar. Blend in egg whites, then add spices and soda, mixing well. Mix in flour, oats and oat bran, beating well.

Drop cookies 2" apart on a non-stick cookie sheet. Bake at 375° for 8 minutes. Cool 1 to 2 minutes on cookie sheet, then remove to a rack to cool.

Yield: 3 dozen; 1 serving = 1 cookie

Per serving:	Calories	Fat (g)	Cholesterol (mg)	Fiber (g)	Sodium (mg)
	83	4	0	1	78

Oatmeal Cookies

2/3 cup soft margarine
2/3 cup brown sugar
2 egg whites
1 tsp. vanilla
11/3 cups unbleached flour *or*
  1 cup unbleached flour plus
  1/3 cup whole wheat flour

1/4 cup oat bran
1/2 tsp. *each* baking soda and cinnamon
1/4 tsp. nutmeg
2 cups rolled oats

Cream together margarine and brown sugar in a large bowl. Beat in egg whites and vanilla.

Mix together flour, oat bran, soda and spices. Gradually add dry ingredients to creamed mixture, mixing well after each addition. (May add up to 1/4 cup water or non-fat milk if batter is too thick.) Stir in oats. Drop by teaspoonfuls onto an ungreased cookie sheet 11/2" apart. Bake at 375° for 12 to 15 minutes. Remove from cookie sheet immediately and cool on a wire rack.

Yield: 5 to 6 dozen; 1 serving = 1 cookie

Per serving:	Calories	Fat (g)	Cholesterol (mg)	Fiber (g)	Sodium (mg)
	39	2	0	0	30

Bread Pudding

1/2 cup raisins
1/4 cup Amaretto, cream sherry,
    bourbon, rum *or* apple juice
6 slices stale whole wheat bread, cubed
1 12-oz. can evaporated non-fat milk
1 cup non-fat milk

1 egg
3 egg whites
1/3 cup brown sugar
1 tsp. cinnamon
1/2 tsp. nutmeg
1 tsp. vanilla

Soak raisins in Amaretto for one hour to soften. Place bread cubes in a 1 1/2 quart baking dish coated with cooking spray. Blend milk, egg, egg whites, sugar, spices and vanilla. Drain liquor from raisins and add to egg mixture. Mix raisins with bread cubes. Pour egg mixture over all. Bake for one hour at 325°.

Variation: Add 4 chopped (unpeeled) apples to bread cubes.

Serves 6 to 8

Per serving:	Calories	Fat (g)	Cholesterol (mg)	Fiber (g)	Sodium (mg)
	185	2	30	2	200

Apple Rice Pudding

1 cup boiling water
1/2 cup chopped dried apricots
2 cups cooked brown rice
1 1/2 cups non-fat milk

2 cups diced, unpeeled apples
1/2 tsp. cinnamon
1/4 tsp. *each* nutmeg and allspice
1 Tbsp. canola *or* safflower oil

Pour water over apricots and soak 30 minutes. Drain well. Mix with remaining ingredients. Pour into a 1 1/2 quart baking dish coated with cooking spray. Bake at 325° for 1 hour.

Serves 4 to 6

Per serving:	Calories	Fat (g)	Cholesterol (mg)	Fiber (g)	Sodium (mg)
	171	3	1	4	220

Apple Crisp

2 Tbsp. *each* canola or safflower oil
2 Tbsp. honey
2¹/2 cups rolled oats
¹/4 cup whole wheat flour
2 tsp. cinnamon
1 tsp. allspice

¹/2 tsp. nutmeg
8 cooking apples, peeled and sliced
1 cup raisins
1 Tbsp. lemon juice
2 tsp. vanilla
¹/2 cup apple *or* orange juice (more if needed)

Combine oil with honey. Mix together with oats, flour, 1 tsp. cinnamon, ¹/2 tsp. allspice and ¹/4 tsp. nutmeg. Mix apple slices with raisins, lemon juice, vanilla and remaining spices.

Coat a 9" x 13" baking pan with cooking spray. Spread ¹/2 of the apple mixture in the pan; top with ¹/2 of the oat mixture. Repeat. Pour on the apple or orange juice. Bake at 325° for 45 minutes or until topping is crisp. Add more juice as necessary during cooking.

Serves 6 to 8

Per serving:	Calories	Fat (g)	Cholesterol (mg)	Fiber (g)	Sodium (mg)
	301	6	0	9	8

Blueberry Oat Squares

1³/4 cups rolled oats
1¹/2 cups whole wheat flour
3/4 cup brown sugar
1 tsp. cinnamon
¹/2 tsp. nutmeg
¹/2 tsp. baking soda
¹/2 cup liquid margarine

4 cups fresh *or* frozen blueberries
¹/4 cup brown sugar
1 tsp. lemon zest
4 Tbsp. water
2 Tbsp. cornstarch
2 tsp. fresh lemon juice

In a medium bowl, combine oats, flour, 3/4 cup brown sugar, cinnamon, nutmeg and baking soda. Add margarine and mix until crumbly. Reserve one cup of mixture for topping. Spread remaining oat mixture over bottom of 9" x 13" baking dish coated with cooking spray. Bake for 10 minutes at 350'.

Meanwhile, combine blueberries, ¹/4 cup brown sugar, zest and 3 Tbsp. water in a medium saucepan. Bring to a boil; simmer 2 to 3 minutes, stirring occasionally. Combine remaining 1 Tbsp. water with cornstarch and lemon juice; mix well. Stir into blueberry mixture; cook and stir until thickened, about 1 minute. Spread over partially baked crust to within 1/4 inch of the edge. Sprinkle with reserved crust mixture. Bake 20 minutes or until topping is crisp. Cool pan on a wire rack then cut into squares.

Yield: 15 squares; 1 serving = 1 square

Per serving:	Calories	Fat (g)	Cholesterol (mg)	Fiber (g)	Sodium (mg)
	205	7	3	2	113

Apple Pie

4 large Golden Delicious apples	1 recipe HealthMark Pie Crust (page 140)
1/3 to 1/2 cup brown *or* white sugar	Non-fat milk
1 tsp. cinnamon	Sugar
1/2 tsp. nutmeg	Cinnamon

Peel, core and slice apples. In a large bowl, combine apple slices with sugar, cinnamon and nutmeg. Roll out crust and place in a pie pan. Fill with apples and cover with top crust. Cut several slits in top to allow steam to escape.

Brush crust with non-fat milk and sprinkle with a mixture of sugar and cinnamon. Bake at 400° for about 40 minutes or until pastry is lightly browned.

Yield: One pie (8 slices); 1 serving = 1 slice

Per serving:	Calories	Fat (g)	Cholesterol (mg)	Fiber (g)	Sodium (mg)
	306	14	0	3	8

Fruit 'n' Yogurt Pie

1 envelope unflavored gelatin	1 banana, sliced
1 to 2 Tbsp. brown sugar	1 tsp. vanilla *or* coconut extract
1/4 cup frozen orange juice concentrate, thawed	1 Graham Cracker Crust, pre-baked (page 170)
2 cups plain non-fat yogurt	
1/2 cup canned, crushed pineapple (juice pack), undrained	

Combine gelatin and brown sugar. Sprinkle over orange juice. Let stand 2 to 3 minutes to soften. Cook over medium heat, stirring constantly, until sugar and gelatin are dissolved.

In a medium bowl, combine yogurt, pineapple and banana. Add gelatin mixture and vanilla; blend well.

Pour into cooled crust. Cover and refrigerate until firm, at least 4 hours or overnight. Decorate with fruit before serving, if desired.

Serves 8

Per serving:	Calories	Fat (g)	Cholesterol (mg)	Fiber (g)	Sodium (mg)
	199	5	4	1	223

English Apple Pie

1/2 cup soft margarine
1/2 cup brown sugar
1 cup all-purpose flour
3/4 cup rolled oats

1/4 cup wheat germ
2 tsp. cinnamon, divided
5 to 6 Golden Delicious apples,
    peeled, cored and sliced

Cream together margarine and sugar. Beat in flour, oatmeal, wheat germ and 1 tsp. cinnamon.

Mix remaining teaspoon of cinnamon with apples. Place apples in a pie pan. Sprinkle oatmeal mixture over the top.

Bake at 375° for 40 to 45 minutes. Serve warm.

Serves 6 to 8

Per serving:	Calories	Fat (g)	Cholesterol (mg)	Fiber (g)	Sodium (mg)
	306	13	0	4	155

HealthMark Pumpkin Pie

1 16-oz. can pumpkin
1 13-oz. can evaporated non-fat milk
3 egg whites
1/2 cup brown sugar
1 tsp. vanilla

1 tsp. cinnamon
1/2 tsp. nutmeg
1/4 tsp. cloves
1 9" Graham Cracker Crust,
    unbaked (page 170)

Combine all ingredients and beat well. Pour into unbaked crust and bake at 375° for 50 to 60 minutes. Let cool slightly before slicing.

Serves 12

Per serving:	Calories	Fat (g)	Cholesterol (mg)	Fiber (g)	Sodium (mg)
	151	3	1	1	173

Graham Cracker Crust

1¹/4 cups graham cracker crumbs *
2 Tbsp. liquid margarine

¹/8 tsp. nutmeg *or* ¹/2 tsp.
orange zest

Combine ingredients and mix well. Press onto bottom and sides of a 9" pie pan. Bake at 375° for 10 minutes.

*Note: Select a brand made with non-hydrogenated oil (e.g. Health Valley or Mi-del)

Yield: 1 bottom crust; 1 serving = ¹/8 of crust

Per serving:	Calories	Fat (g)	Cholesterol (mg)	Fiber (g)	Sodium (mg)
	109	5	0	1	180

HealthMark Pie Crust

2 cups unbleached *or*
   whole wheat pastry flour
Pinch Lite Salt™ (optional)

¹/2 cup canola *or* safflower oil
¹/4 cup non-fat milk *or* cold water

In a medium bowl or in a food processor, combine flour and salt. Pour in oil and milk then until crumbly. Gather together in a ball. Divide in half and roll out each half between two sheets of wax paper. Handle carefully.

Yield: One top and bottom crust; 1 serving = ¹/8 of crust

Per serving:	Calories	Fat (g)	Cholesterol (mg)	Fiber (g)	Sodium (mg)
	228	14	0	1	4

Angel Food Cake

1 cup sugar
12 egg whites (1¹/2 cups), divided
²/3 cup boiling water
1 tsp. almond extract

¹/2 cup canola *or* safflower oil
1¹/2 cups unbleached flour
2¹/2 tsp. baking powder
¹/2 tsp. cream of tartar

Process sugar in food processor until finely ground. Remove and divide in half.

Place ¹/2 cup egg whites, water, extract and oil in work bowl and process for 2 minutes. Sift flour, baking powder and remaining ¹/2 cup sugar. Add to work bowl and process 4 minutes.

Meanwhile in a large bowl, beat remaining 1 cup egg whites until frothy. Add cream of tartar and beat until stiff, then gradually beat in remaining ¹/2 cup sugar, to form a meringue.

Fold flour mixture into meringue until well combined. Pour batter into an ungreased angel food cake pan and bake at 350° for 50 minutes. Invert pan over a bottle and cool completely before removing cake from pan. Serve with Basic Fruit Sauce (page 77) or sliced fresh fruit.

Serves 12 to 16

Per serving:	Calories	Fat (g)	Cholesterol (mg)	Fiber (g)	Sodium (mg)
	210	9	0	0	135

Mincemeat Gingerbread

1 9-oz package condensed mincemeat
1 cup water
¹/2 cup canola *or* safflower oil
¹/3 cup brown sugar
2 egg whites

2 cups whole wheat flour
1 tsp. *each* baking soda,
 cinnamon and ginger
¹/2 tsp. cloves
³/4 cup *each* molasses and hot water

Combine mincemeat and 1 cup water in a 1 quart pan. Bring to boil and cook, stirring, for 1 to 2 minutes. Spread evenly into a 9" x 13" pan coated with cooking spray.

Beat together oil, sugar and egg whites. Blend flour, soda and spices. Mix together molasses and 3/4 cup hot water. Alternately add flour and molasses mixtures to oil mixture. Beat well. Spread over mincemeat.

Bake at 325° for 40 to 50 minutes or until top springs back when touched. Cool 10 minutes. Loosen edges and invert into a platter. Cool at least 20 minutes. Serve warm or at room temperature with Whipped Topping (page 182).

Yield: One 9" x 13" cake; 12 servings

Per serving:	Calories	Fat (g)	Cholesterol (mg)	Fiber (g)	Sodium (mg)
	277	10	0	2	157

Cranberry-Orange Cake

2¹/2 cups unbleached flour
3/4 cup sugar
1 tsp. baking powder
1 tsp. baking soda
1/2 cup walnuts *or* pecans
1 cup chopped dates *or* 1 cup chopped
   apricots (may be soaked for several
   hours in brandy, Amaretto or another
   liqueur

1 cup whole cranberries
1 Tbsp. orange zest
4 egg whites
1 cup low-fat buttermilk
1/2 cup canola *or* safflower oil

Optional topping:
1/2 cup sugar
1 cup orange juice

In a large bowl, blend together dry ingredients. Stir in nuts, dried fruit, cranberries and orange zest. In a separate bowl, beat together egg whites, buttermilk and oil. Stir into flour mixture until well blended. Pour into a non-stick bundt or tube pan coated with cooking spray. Bake at 350° for 50 to 60 minutes or until cake tester comes out clean.

Remove from oven and cool in pan for 15 minutes. Turn out onto a cake rack to cool completely.

Sprinkle with powdered sugar or drizzle with topping: heat sugar and orange juice together until sugar dissolves. Pour over cake. Scrape up drippings and pour over cake several times for an attractive glaze.

Yield: 1 bundt cake, 12 servings

Per serving:	Calories	Fat (g)	Cholesterol (mg)	Fiber (g)	Sodium (mg)
	304	13	0	2	146

Carrot Cake

1¹/2 cups whole wheat flour
1¹/2 cups unbleached flour
¹/2 cup brown sugar
2¹/2 tsp. baking soda
1 Tbsp. cinnamon
2 cups shredded carrots
1 cup crushed pineapple (juice pack), undrained

1 cup honey
¹/2 cup canola or safflower oil
4 egg whites
1 Tbsp. vanilla
¹/3 cup walnuts (optional)
Orange Cream Cheese Frosting (recipe follows)

In a large bowl, combine all ingredients and beat for 2 minutes at high speed. Pour into a 9"x13" baking pan coated with cooking spray. Bake at 350° for 40 to 50 minutes or until cake tester comes out clean. Cool in pan for 30 minutes. Frost with Orange Cream Cheese Frosting.

Yield: 1 9"x13" cake (12 servings)

Per serving:	Calories	Fat (g)	Cholesterol (mg)	Fiber (g)	Sodium (mg)
	430	14	14	2	345

Orange Cream Cheese Frosting

8 ounces light cream cheese
8 ounces Weight Watchers™ Creamed Cheese
¹/3 cup honey

3 Tbsp. orange juice concentrate, thawed
2 tsp. lemon juice
1 Tbsp. orange zest

Beat all ingredients together until smooth. Chill 1 hour before frosting cake.

Yield: 1¹/2 cups; 1 serving = 2 Tbsp.

Per serving:	Calories	Fat (g)	Cholesterol (mg)	Fiber (g)	Sodium (mg)
	97	5	16	0	153

Carrot Fruitcake

1 cup grated carrots
3/4 cup raisins
1/2 cup apple juice concentrate, thawed
1 cup water
2 Tbsp. canola *or* safflower oil
1 cup unbleached flour

1/2 cup whole wheat flour
1 tsp. *each* cinnamon and allspice
1/2 tsp. baking soda
1/2 cup wheat germ
1/4 cup chopped walnuts
1 1/2 cups cranberries (optional)

Mix together carrots, raisins, apple juice concentrate, water and oil. Blend flours, spices, soda, wheat germ, nuts and cranberries (if used). Combine the two mixtures and mix well. Pour into two 9" x 5" loaf pans coated with cooking spray. Bake at 300° for 45 minutes.

Yield: Two 9" x 5" loaves, 32 slices; 1 serving = 1 slice

Per serving:	Calories	Fat (g)	Cholesterol (mg)	Fiber (g)	Sodium (mg)
	57	2	0	1	16

Denise's Date Loaf

4 egg whites
1/2 cup brown sugar
8 oz. dates, chopped
1 cup boiling water
1/2 cup canola *or* safflower oil

2 cups whole wheat flour
1 tsp. ginger
1 tsp. orange zest
1 tsp. *each* baking soda and baking powder

Beat together egg whites and brown sugar. Mix dates, boiling water and oil; blend with egg white mixture.

Combine dry ingredients. Add egg white mixture, mixing until just combined. Turn batter into a 9" x 5" loaf pan coated with cooking spray. Bake at 350° for 1 hour.

Yield: One 9" x 5" loaf, 16 slices; 1 serving = 1 slice

Per serving:	Calories	Fat (g)	Cholesterol (mg)	Fiber (g)	Sodium (mg)
	179	7	0	2	92

Orange Date Gingerbread

1 cup whole wheat flour
1 1/2 cups unbleached flour
1 tsp. *each* baking soda and baking powder
1 tsp. cinnamon
1/2 tsp. *each* ginger and cloves

1/2 cup chopped dates
1/2 cup chopped candied orange peel
2 egg whites
1/4 cup canola *or* safflower oil
1/2 cup *each* orange juice and non-fat milk
3/4 cup molasses

Mix together flours, baking soda, baking powder and spices. Fold in dates and orange zest.

In a separate bowl, beat together egg whites, oil, juice, milk and molasses. Stir this into flour mixture and blend well.

Pour into a 9" x 5" loaf pan coated with cooking spray and bake at 350° for 40 to 45 minutes (or use an 8" x 8" baking pan and bake for 30 to 35 minutes).

Yield: One 9" x 5" loaf, 16 slices; 1 serving = 1 slice

Per serving:	Calories	Fat (g)	Cholesterol (mg)	Fiber (g)	Sodium (mg)
	169	4	0	2	91

Cappucino Parfait

1 pkg. unflavored gelatin
2 1/4 cups strong, decaffeinated coffee, divided
1/4 cup brown sugar

1 cup evaporated non-fat milk
1 tsp. vanilla
2 Tbsp. Kahlua *or* other coffee-flavored liqueur (optional)

Combine gelatin and 1/2 cup coffee in a small bowl; let stand 1 minute.

Heat remaining coffee to a simmer in a small saucepan. Add gelatin mixture and sugar to hot coffee. Cook over low heat, stirring constantly, until gelatin and sugar dissolve. Remove from heat; stir in evaporated milk and vanilla. Cool. Pour into 8" x 8" pan. Freeze until almost solid.

Spoon mixture into blender or food processor. Add liqueur and process until smooth. Return to pan and freeze until firm. Spoon into parfait glasses and serve immediately.

Serves 4

Per serving:	Calories	Fat (g)	Cholesterol (mg)	Fiber (g)	Sodium (mg)
	128	0	3	0	24

Chocolate Sherbet

1³/₄ cups cocoa powder
1 cup brown sugar
¹/₈ tsp. salt

3¹/₂ cups non-fat milk
2 tsp. vanilla

Combine cocoa, sugar and salt in a saucepan. Gradually stir in milk and vanilla. Over medium heat bring just to a boil, stirring constantly. Continue stirring and simmer for 5 minutes. Cool, then pour into a shallow pan and freeze.

Spoon into food processor or blender and process until smooth. Serve immediately.

Yield: Ten ¹/₂ cup servings

Per serving:	Calories	Fat (g)	Cholesterol (mg)	Fiber (g)	Sodium (mg)
	167	1	2	0	147

Frozen Fruit Yogurt

1 16 to 20-oz. bag frozen unsweetened
   strawberries (*or* other frozen fruit)
1 cup plain non-fat yogurt

2 to 3 Tbsp. brown sugar, honey
   or 2 to 3 pkgs. Equal

Place fruit in food processor fitted with a metal blade. Pulse three times, then process continuously until fruit is finely chopped. Scrape down sides of work bowl as necessary.

Add yogurt and sugar or Equal. Process until smooth and creamy. Serve immediately or freeze tightly covered.

Yield: 3 cups; 1 serving = ¹/₂ cup

Per serving:	Calories	Fat (g)	Cholesterol (mg)	Fiber (g)	Sodium (mg)
	74	1	2	0	30

Frozen Orange Cream

2 cups non-fat milk
2 Tbsp. brown sugar
1 6-oz. can frozen orange juice
    concentrate, thawed
1 1/2 tsp. orange zest

Combine milk, sugar, juice and zest. Stir until sugar is dissolved. Pour into a shallow pan and freeze.

Spoon into food processor or blender and process until smooth. Serve in sherbet glasses or in lemon halves with pulp removed.

Yield: Five 1/2 cup servings

Per serving:	Calories	Fat (g)	Cholesterol (mg)	Fiber (g)	Sodium (mg)
	107	0	2	0	53

Orange-Banana Mousse

2 pkgs. unflavored gelatin
2/3 cup hot water
1/4 cup brown sugar
1 6-oz. can frozen orange juice
    concentrate

1 cup plain non-fat yogurt
1 tsp. vanilla
1 banana, peeled and cut into chunks
6 ice cubes, crushed

Put gelatin and hot water in blender or food processor and process until well blended, about 15 seconds. Add sugar and process for 30 seconds longer. Add **frozen** juice concentrate, yogurt, vanilla and banana, and process until pureed. With machine running, add crushed ice a little at a time and process until mixture is smooth, about 45 seconds.

Immediately pour into 6 serving dishes. Chill until firm, about 30 minutes.

Variation: Substitute 12 large frozen strawberries for ice cubes. May use other frozen fruit also.

Serves 6

Per serving:	Calories	Fat (g)	Cholesterol (mg)	Fiber (g)	Sodium (mg)
	127	1	2	0	33

Raspberry Yogurt Parfait

1 egg white
1 to 2 Tbsp. brown sugar
1 cup plain non-fat yogurt
1 Tbsp. orange flavored liqueur *or*
  thawed frozen orange juice concentrate

1 12-oz. pkg. frozen raspberries
  (sugar-free), thawed and drained

Beat egg white until stiff. Gradually add brown sugar, beating until glossy. Fold in remaining ingredients. Spoon into serving glasses.

Serves 4

Per serving:	Calories	Fat (g)	Cholesterol (mg)	Fiber (g)	Sodium (mg)
	115	2	3	4	54

Instant Sorbet

A terrific dessert — ready in an instant

1 20-oz. can crushed pineapple,
  packed in juice

3 nectarines *or* peaches
1 cup strawberries, fresh or frozen

Pour pineapple into a zip-top plastic bag. Add remaining fruit and freeze. Thaw slightly before using. Place fruit in food processor and process until smooth and creamy (like frozen yogurt).

Serve immediately or spread mixture into an 8" x 8" pan and freeze solid. Thaw enough to break into chunks. Process again in food processor or blender. Freeze mixture until firm, then serve.

Variations:

• Use seasonal fruit of your choice.

• Add 1 cup plain non-fat yogurt and 1 to 2 Tbsp. brown sugar or 2 to 3 pkgs. Equal to pureed fruit. Amount of sweetener used depends on ripeness of the fruit. Use as little as possible.

Serves 6

Per serving:	Calories	Fat (g)	Cholesterol (mg)	Fiber (g)	Sodium (mg)
	85	0	0	2	5

Frozen Banana Ice

4 bananas, peeled and frozen
1 cup plain non-fat yogurt

2 tsp. vanilla
1/4 tsp. nutmeg

Place all ingredients in food processor or blender. Process until smooth and creamy. Serve at once or chill in freezer for up to one hour. May also be frozen; thaw for one hour in refrigerator before serving.

Serves 4 to 6

Per serving:	Calories	Fat (g)	Cholesterol (mg)	Fiber (g)	Sodium (mg)
	96	1	2	1	27

Strawberry Amaretto Fluff

3 egg whites at room temperature
1/4 tsp. cream of tartar
1/4 tsp. vanilla
1 tsp. lemon juice

1 Tbsp. Amaretto
1 Tbsp. brown sugar *or*
  2 pkgs. Equal
2 cups hulled strawberries, diced

Beat egg whites and cream of tartar until soft peaks form. Add vanilla, lemon juice, Amaretto and sugar. Continue beating until stiff. Fold in strawberries. Chill before serving.

Serves 6

Per serving:	Calories	Fat (g)	Cholesterol (mg)	Fiber (g)	Sodium (mg)
	40	0	0	1	26

Strawberry Meringue

2 egg whites
2 cups ripe strawberries (may
    substitute other fruit)

1/4 cup brown sugar
1 tsp. *each* lemon juice and vanilla

Combine all ingredients in food processor work bowl fitted with a steel knife. Process until light and frothy. Freeze.

Serves 4 to 6

Per serving:	Calories	Fat (g)	Cholesterol (mg)	Fiber (g)	Sodium (mg)
	59	0	0	1	20

Yogurt Fluff

1 pkg. fruit flavored gelatin
    (regular or sugar-free)
1 cup plain non-fat yogurt

Prepare gelatin according to package directions. Chill until syrupy. Beat in yogurt. Refrigerate until firm.

Variation: Add 1 cup unsweetened fruit.

Serves 6

Per serving:	Calories	Fat (g)	Cholesterol (mg)	Fiber (g)	Sodium (mg)
	71	1	2	0	26

Orange Baked Pears

2 Bartlett pears
1/2 cup orange juice
1 Tbsp. raisins
1 tsp. orange zest

1 tsp. cornstarch
1/4 tsp. cinnamon
Dash allspice

Cut pears in half lengthwise and core. Pierce inside of pear halves with a fork. Arrange cut side up in a baking dish.

Combine orange juice, raisins, orange zest, cornstarch and spices. Cook over medium heat, stirring frequently, until thickened. Pour glaze over pear halves.

Bake at 325° for 20 to 30 minutes or until easily pierced with a fork. Baste several times with glaze during cooking.

Serves 4

	Calories	Fat (g)	Cholesterol (mg)	Fiber (g)	Sodium (mg)
Per serving:	74	0	0	2	3

Yogurt Topping

1 cup plain non-fat yogurt
1 to 2 tsp. brown sugar, honey *or*
  2 pkgs. Equal

1 tsp. vanilla, orange *or* lemon extract
2 tsp. chopped fresh mint (optional)

Blend all ingredients and chill before serving.

Yield: 1 cup; 1 serving = 2 Tbsp.

	Calories	Fat (g)	Cholesterol (mg)	Fiber (g)	Sodium (mg)
Per serving:	24	0	2	0	20

Whipped Topping One

1/2 cup ice water *or* fruit juice*
1 tsp. fresh lemon juice
2 tsp. vanilla

1/2 cup non-fat dry milk
2 to 3 Tbsp. sugar

Chill a small bowl and beaters for mixer. Mix water (or juice), lemon juice and vanilla. Stir in dry milk and beat until thick, 5 to 7 minutes. Gradually beat in sugar.

Serve over fresh fruit or other desserts in place of whipped cream. Serve immediately; does not keep well

* Use orange juice and Grand Marnier (optional) or apple juice and Calvados (optional) — delicious on a baked apple — or cranberry juice and Chambord (optional)

Yield: about 2 cups; 1 serving = 2 Tbsp.

Per serving:	Calories	Fat (g)	Cholesterol (mg)	Fiber (g)	Sodium (mg)
	42	0	2	0	40

Whipped Topping Two

1 cup evaporated non-fat milk
1/4 cup sugar
1 1/2 tsp. vanilla

Pour milk into a medium bowl and chill until ice crystals form around the edges and mixture is slushy. Chill beaters. Beat milk on high speed until fluffy. Add remaining ingredients and beat until stiff. Serve immediately; does not keep well.

Variation: Sprinkle 1 tsp. gelatin over 2 Tbsp. water in a small saucepan. Stir over low heat until dissolved. Do not chill milk. Add dissolved gelatin to milk and beat until stiff. Beat in remaining ingredients. This topping may be kept in refrigerator until ready to serve.

Yield: about 4 cups; 1 serving = 2 Tbsp.

Per serving:	Calories	Fat (g)	Cholesterol (mg)	Fiber (g)	Sodium (mg)
	12	0	0	0	9

Cranberry Candy

A sparkling bright holiday treat

2 cups (about 1/2 lb.) cranberries
11/2 Tbsp. orange zest
3/4 cup orange juice

3/4 cup brown sugar
3 pkgs. unflavored gelatin
1/3 cup chopped walnuts

Combine cranberries, orange zest and juice. Cook over medium heat for about 15 minutes or until cranberries soften and pop open; cool.

Puree cooled mixture in a blender or food processor. Combine puree, sugar and gelatin in a saucepan. Cook over medium-high heat for 10 to 15 minutes or until you can see the pan for a full second when spoon is drawn across. Stir in nuts.

Spread mixture evenly in a 9" x 5" loaf pan coated with cooking spray and let stand, uncovered, overnight. Cut into 1" squares.

Yield: about 15 squares; 1 serving = 1 square

Per serving:	Calories	Fat (g)	Cholesterol (mg)	Fiber (g)	Sodium (mg)
	75	2	0	1	5

Cooking for a Healthier Ever After

ORDER FORM

Send to: HealthMark Centers, Inc., 5801 So. Quebec, Suite 100
Englewood, CO 80111; (303) 694-5060

NAME_____ TELEPHONE_____ (day) _____(eve)

STREET ADDRESS_____

CITY/STATE/ZIP _____

	Quantity	Price	Tax*	Total
Delitefully HealthMark	_____	$16.95	$ 1.13 per book	_____
Cooking for a Healthier Ever After	_____	$16.95	$ 1.13 per book	_____
The HealthMark Program for Life	_____	$18.95	$ 1.26 per book	_____

Plus $2.50 shipping and handling per book _____

TOTAL ENCLOSED _____

Please make checks payable to: Healthmark Centers, Inc. Please do not send cash. Sorry, no COD's.

* Colorado Residents only

- -

ORDER FORM

Send to: HealthMark Centers, Inc., 5801 So. Quebec, Suite 100
Englewood, CO 80111; (303) 694-5060

NAME_____ TELEPHONE_____ (day) _____(eve)

STREET ADDRESS_____

CITY/STATE/ZIP _____

	Quantity	Price	Tax*	Total
Delitefully HealthMark	_____	$16.95	$ 1.13 per book	_____
Cooking for a Healthier Ever After	_____	$16.95	$ 1.13 per book	_____
The HealthMark Program for Life	_____	$18.95	$ 1.26 per book	_____

Plus $2.50 shipping and handling per book _____

TOTAL ENCLOSED _____

Please make checks payable to: Healthmark Centers, Inc. Please do not send cash. Sorry, no COD's.

* Colorado Residents only

Index

Index

Index

Index

The HealthMark Philosophy

The HealthMark cookbooks, *Cooking for a Healthier Ever After* and *Delitefully HealthMark*, were created by Susan Stevens, M.A., R.D., Director of Nutrition at HealthMark to help graduates of the HealthMark preventive medicine programs maintain their healthy lifestyle. Recipes were developed according to HealthMark dietary guidelines to be low in fat, cholesterol, sodium and calories.

Current medical research clearly shows the relationship between diet, lifestyle and disease. Eight of the leading causes of death in the United States are related to poor dietary habits, lack of exercise, smoking and stress: heart disease, stroke, high blood pressure, adult onset diabetes, lung, colon, breast and prostate cancer

A healthy diet, regular exercise and stress reduction can significantly delay — or often prevent — the onset of these diseases.

HealthMark Centers, Inc. is a preventive medicine clinic founded in 1985 in Denver, Colorado by Dr. Robert A. Gleser in response to the need for education about lifestyle changes to lower risk for life-threatening disease. To date, over 10,000 people have completed one of HealthMark's preventive medicine/education programs and are leading healthier lives as a result. The programs focus on what you CAN eat and still reduce your intake of fat, cholesterol, sodium and calories. We offer positive programs for a lifetime of good health.

Supermarket shelf-labeling programs and a successful restaurant program help graduates — as well as the community — make healthier food choices. The ease and convenience of these programs motivate and help many people maintain their newly developed eating and exercise habits.

If you would like to know more about the exciting programs offered at HealthMark, please send us the card below.

☐ Please send more information about the HealthMark Programs

☐ Please have a HealthMark representative call me

Name _____

Street Address _____

City/State/Zip _____

Telephone: Day_____ Evening_____

HealthMark Centers, Inc. • Associated with Saint Joseph Hospital
5801 South Quebec, Suite 100 • Englewood, Colorado 80111 • (303) 694-5060

Return Address Information

_____
_____
_____

HealthMark Centers, Inc.
5801 So. Quebec, Suite 100
Englewood, CO 80111